MODERN MILITARY AIRCRAFT

DEVELOPMENT • WEAPONRY • SPECIFICATIONS

00
8873
NAVY
USS JOHN F KENNEDY
5-38
VS24

MODERN MILITARY AIRCRAFT

DEVELOPMENT • WEAPONRY • SPECIFICATIONS

Robert Jackson

CHARTWELL BOOKS, INC.

Published by
CHARTWELL BOOKS, INC.
A Division of **BOOK SALES, INC.**
114 Northfield Avenue
Edison, New Jersey 08837

ISBN 0-7858-1695-X

Editorial and Design by
Amber Books Ltd
Bradley's Close
74–77 White Lion Street
London N1 9PF
www.amberbooks.co.uk

Project Editor: James Bennett
Design: Zoe Mellors

Printed in Singapore

PICTURE CREDITS

All artworks © Aerospace Publishing Ltd

All photographs © TRH Pictures except
Aerospace Publishing:
6,7,8,11,12,13,61,65,72,73,76,81,88,96,197,269,284,
296,312,313

Contents

INTRODUCTION

In the immediate post-World War II years, the awesome destructive power of nuclear weapons dominated air power doctrine to such an extent that many of the tactical air power lessons, learned the hard way during World War II, were forgotten.

Yet the war that erupted in Korea in June 1950 required the use of tactical air power on a scale not seen since the Battle of Normandy, for it was the United Nations' only means of blunting the North Korean offensive during the crucial early weeks of the conflict. The brunt of the ground-attack work, initially, was borne by piston-engined types that had excelled themselves in World War II, the Mustang and Corsair, but the real workhorse of the campaign was the Lockheed F-80 Shooting Star, America's first operational jet fighter-bomber. More than adequate for ground attack, the F-80 was, however, no match in air combat for the swept-wing MiG-15, which appeared in Korean skies in November 1950. It was countered by the North American F-86 Sabre, the two types battling for supremacy over northwest

A Lockheed F-80 Shooting Star departs a Chinese airfield during the Korean war.

RAF Lightnings often intercepted Soviet 'Bear' aircraft during the Cold War.

Korea in history's first jet-versus-jet battles. For the most part, the MiGs were flown by Russians, whole fighter divisions and regiments being assigned to bases in Manchuria for combat duty.

The Korean War had a dramatic effect on the organization and equipment of both the USAF and the Soviet Air Force. Strategic Air Command, which had already begun re-equipping some of its B-29 medium bomber wings with the improved B-50 when hostilities broke out, now quickly phased out the rest of its B-29 bombers, converting some to the flight refuelling tanker role, and by the end of 1954 they had been entirely replaced by the Boeing B-47 Stratojet. In 1955 the heavy bomber wings, then equipped with the huge Convair B-36, began to re-equip with the Boeing B-52 Stratofortress. To facilitate rapid deployment, and to extend the range of the SAC bomber force, the SAC tanker fleet was also greatly expanded, with orders placed for KC-135 jet tankers to replace the Command's existing KB-50s and KC-97s, both of which had superseded the KB-29s. The Russians, meanwhile, had viewed the losses sustained by the USAF's B-29s over Korea with concern; their sole strategic bomber, the Tupolev Tu-4 'Bull', had been copied from B-29s that had come

USAF U2-As were operated by the 4028th Strategic Reconnaissance Squadron.

down on Soviet territory after raids on Japan in WWII. Late in 1952 the Tupolev design bureau began work on a strategic jet bomber that was to emerge as the Tu-16 'Badger', which was roughly the equivalent of the B-47, and during the next two years two strategic heavy bombers, the Myasischchev Mya-4 'Bison' and the Tupolev Tu-95 'Bear', also made their appearance.

Great changes also swept through the USAF Tactical Air Command as a result of the Korean War. Before the end of 1953 TAC's remaining F-51 and F-80 units had equipped with F-86F fighter-bombers, followed by the nuclear-capable F-86H. By the middle of 1954 TAC's light bomber units had begun to receive the Martin B-57 Canberra, which in turn gave way to the F-100 Super Sabre from 1957. Also in 1954 TAC began to receive swept-wing F-84F Thunderstreaks to replace its Thunderjets, many of which were assigned to European NATO air forces. Later, from the same Republic Aviation stable, came the F-105 Thunderchief, TAC's first true weapons system.

The Russians, always tactically minded,

fielded the Sukhoi Su-7 'Fitter', which replaced ground-attack versions of the MiG-15 and MiG-17 - neither of which was suited to the role - from 1956. The Fitter, which was also widely exported, became the standard Soviet tactical support fighter-bomber, and remained so for two decades in a number of developed versions.

On both sides of the Iron Curtain, three years of jet combat experience over the Yalu was woven into the designs of new air interceptors. In the United States, the agile brain of Lockheed's Clarence Johnson and his design team gave birth to the revolutionary F-104 Starfighter, while Russia's answer was the MiG-21. All-weather fighters, too, assumed high priority; in 1955 the USAF received the first examples of the Convair F-102 Delta Dagger, the outcome of a USAF requirement dating back to 1950, and in the following year Soviet air defence squadrons received the Yakovlev Yak-25 Flashlight. The lessons of Korea were also absorbed by the British, who accelerated deployment of their nuclear deterrent force (the V-force) and ordered fighter types like the Hawker Hunter and Gloster Javelin into 'super-priority' production. Both, eventually, would be replaced by the Mach 2 English Electric Lightning interceptor. The French, too, pushed ahead with the development of their Dassault Mirage family of advanced combat aircraft.

One major problem that had manifested itself in Korea was strategic reconnaissance. The Americans solved it by developing two types of aircraft: the RB-57, a greatly modified high-altitude version of the Canberra, and the purpose-built Lockheed U-2. But it was in two other areas that the Korean war probably had its greatest impact.

The first was in the tactical transport field. Korea had shown the need for a transport aircraft with a large load-carrying capacity that could operate from rough airstrips, and again it was Lockheed that came up with the answer in the C-130 Hercules, the most versatile transport aircraft ever designed.The second involved the multi-role combat aircraft, and here it was the US Navy that provided the lead. The Korean War had proved beyond all doubt that the fast attack carrier was still the most vital unit in modern naval warfare; at the same time, the deficiencies of the Navy's standard jet types - the F9F Panther and the F2H Banshee - over Korea had aroused serious misgivings, and propeller-driven attack types could no longer hope to survive in a hostile fighter environment. These shortcomings gave rise to a US Navy requirement for an aircraft that could take over the task of the Skyraider, carry a substantial weapons load - including nuclear weapons - at a speed twice that of the conventional aircraft, and stand in as an interceptor when the need arose. The result was the remarkable Douglas A-4 Skyhawk, which was rolled out of Douglas's El Segundo factory only nineteen months after its inception and which flew for the first time in June 1954. At the same time, work went ahead on what was to become the world's first multi-role supersonic combat aircraft - the McDonnell F-4 Phantom. Both types were to play a dominant part in Vietnam over a decade later.

The air war over Vietnam, in its turn - in particular the combat experiences of US pilots in action against Russian MiG-21s - produced two requirements, one for a close support aircraft that could operate from primitive sites close to the front line, and the other for an agile combat aircraft. The first was met by the British Harrier V/STOL aircraft, which was further developed by McDonnell Douglas for the US Marine Corps, while the second produced the USAF's McDonnell Douglas

The long-serving Boeing B-52 was still in use over Afghanistan during 2001.

F-15 and the Navy's Grumman F-14 Tomcat. In 1991, the F-15 proved its value as an air superiority fighter over Iraq, where its principal adversary was its Russian-built equivalent, the MiG-29.

During the 1980s, much effort was devoted to finding a replacement for the Fairchild Republic A-10 dedicated battlefield support aircraft, and studies were launched to determine the optimum configuration of a small, agile combat aircraft capable of delivering the widest possible variety of 'smart' weapons and of surviving in the most hostile environment. Fascinating though these studies were, they were negated almost overnight by the experience of the 1991 Gulf War, when the lion's share of the damage to enemy armour was inflicted by fast jets carrying out blistering attacks with huge loads of conventional ordnance, rather than smart weapons, from medium altitude after defence suppression aircraft had dealt with the SAM threat. Furthermore, had the enemy's most modern agile jet fighters appeared to challenge the attacks, most of the attackers were equally as agile, if not more

A pair of C-130 Hercules overflying blazing oilfields during the Gulf War.

so, and could have fought as air-superiority fighters once their air-to-ground weaponry had been released.

The first priority in achieving successful battlefield support, therefore, is to neutralize the enemy's SAM and radar-controlled AAA systems, leaving the way clear for medium-level attacks - beyond the envelope of small arms and shoulder-launched missiles - by large numbers of fast, agile aircraft armed with substantial warloads and equipped with the necessary targeting systems to deliver those loads with great accuracy in all weathers, by day and night. In these circumstances they need not be new, costly or even stealthy aircraft, but they must be aircraft whose basic, inherent design is capable of ongoing development to accommodate new equipment and of meeting the evolving demands of air warfare, one of the fundamental tests of a truly successful weapons system.

One such aircraft is the Lockheed Martin F-16 Fighting Falcon. Designed and built originally by General Dynamics, The F-16 had its origin in a 1972 USAF requirement for a lightweight fighter, and first flew in 1974. Firmly proven in battle with the US and Israeli air forces, the F-16 has been the subject of almost continual development since it first flew, and this pattern is likely to continue for some years to come, for ultra-modern (and ultra-costly) aircraft like the Lockheed Martin F-22 Raptor can never fully replace aircraft in the F-16 category. One of the most exciting proposals entails adapting the aircraft for the uninhabited combat aerial vehicle (UCAV) role; this envisages modifying some of the large number of redundant F-16As held in storage to serve as pilotless long-endurance stand-off weapons carriers, remotely controlled from a distant base.

The principal object of air warfare - to establish air superiority in support of ground operations - has not changed since WWI. What has changed is the mission, which is no longer the defence of national territory or a treaty obligation. Today, elements of the air forces of one or other of the former major power blocs may be called upon to operate anywhere in the world, sometimes in concert with each other, sometimes not, in support of a UN resolution. Aircrews may find themselves locked in combat with aircraft and weapon systems built in their own countries and sold to Third World powers, flown by opponents trained by the same system as themselves.

A USAF F-16 Fighting Falcon refuelling from a tanker aircraft over Kuwait.

CZECH REPUBLIC/SLOVAKIA

AERO L-39 ALBATROS

An excellent design, the Aero L-39 became the standard jet trainer in the air forces of the Warsaw Pact, and was exported as a light attack aircraft.

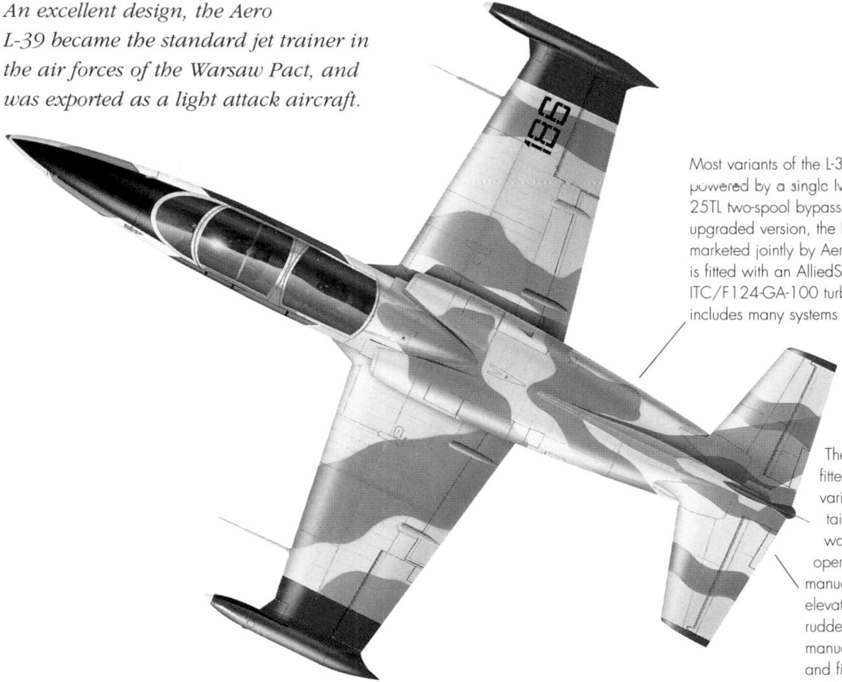

Most variants of the L-39 were powered by a single Ivchonko AI-25TL two-spool bypass turbofan. An upgraded version, the L-159, to be marketed jointly by Aero and Boeing, is fitted with an AlliedSignal ITC/F124-GA-100 turbofan and includes many systems improvements.

The L-39 was fitted with a variable-incidence tailplane that was electrically operated, but with manually operated elevators. The rudder was manually operated, and fitted with a small trim tab.

The L-39C's student and instructor sat in tandem in separate, well-appointed (if somewhat outdated by western standards) cockpits. The aircraft was equipped with Czech-designed rocket-assisted ejection seats which could be used at ground level at speeds in excess of 277km/h (172mph).

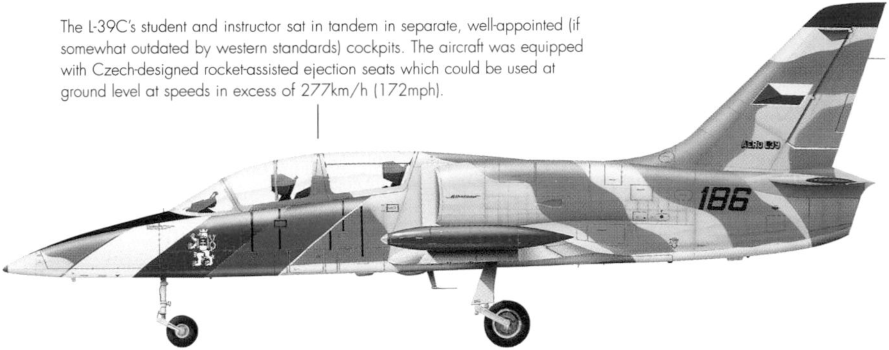

The L-39 was fitted with a simple and robust undercarriage incorporating many features that made it suitable for operation from semi-prepared strips.

Designed to succeed the L-29 as the standard jet trainer in the air forces of Czechoslovakia, the USSR and East Germany, the L-39 Albatros was developed under the leadership of Aero's chief designer, Jan Vleek. A cantilever low wing monoplane, the prototype L-39 first flew in November 1968 and evolved into the L-39C, the standard trainer variant. The aircraft was of all-metal stressed skin structure. The fuselage was of semi-monocoque design, built in two main portions. The front portion housed

First flown in 1968, the L-39 entered service in 1974 with the Czech Air Force.

electrical and radio equipment in the nose and a pressurized compartment for the crew. The rear section, aft of the crew seats, contained fuel tanks and engine bay, and could be quickly removed for rapid servicing. Fitted with a turbofan engine, the L-39 was much more powerful than its predecessor, permitting its use as a light attack aircraft. Two light attack versions were produced: the L-39ZO single-seater, and the L-39ZA, which retained the original two-seat configuration.

Aero L-39C

Type:	single/two-seat trainer/light attack aircraft
Powerplant:	one 1720kg (3793lb) thrust Ivchenko AI-25TL turbofan
Performance:	maximum speed 630km/h (391mph) at 5000m (16,404ft); service ceiling 9000m (29,525ft); range 1750km (1087 miles)
Weights:	empty 3330kg (7341lb); maximum take-off 5270kg (11,618lb)
Dimensions:	wing span 9.46m (31ft); length 12.32m (40ft 5in); height 4.72m (15ft 5.5in)
Armament:	one 23mm (0.906in) twin-barrel cannon; 2 AAMs; 57 or 130mm (2.24 or 5.12in) rocket pods; bombs up to 500kg (1102lb)

Shown here is the single-seat Aero L-39ZA, a light attack variant.

FRANCE

DASSAULT MIRAGE F.1

France's Dassault company has always been prepared to risk privately funded ventures, and the risk has been amply justified by its export record. The Mirage F.1 was one of its major success stories.

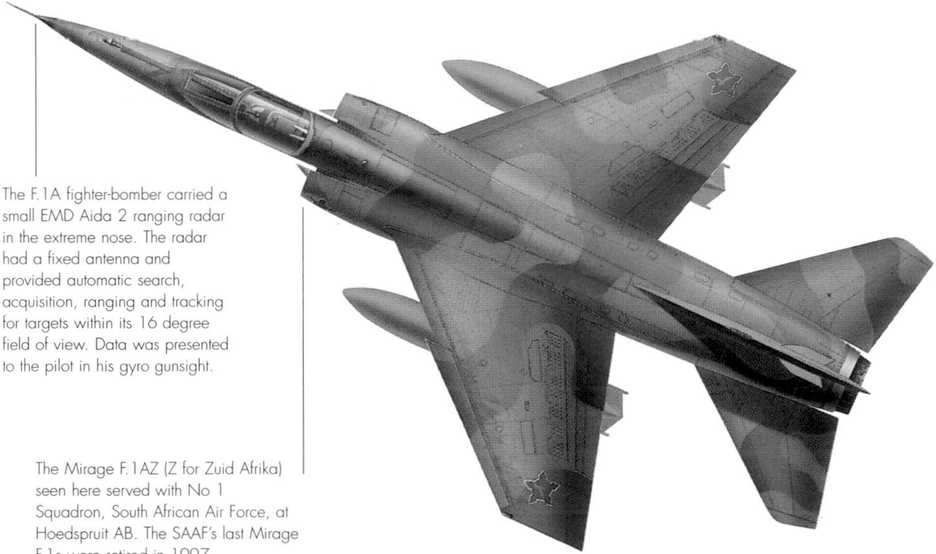

The F.1A fighter-bomber carried a small EMD Aida 2 ranging radar in the extreme nose. The radar had a fixed antenna and provided automatic search, acquisition, ranging and tracking for targets within its 16 degree field of view. Data was presented to the pilot in his gyro gunsight.

The Mirage F.1AZ (Z for Zuid Afrika) seen here served with No 1 Squadron, South African Air Force, at Hoedspruit AB. The SAAF's last Mirage F.1s were retired in 1997.

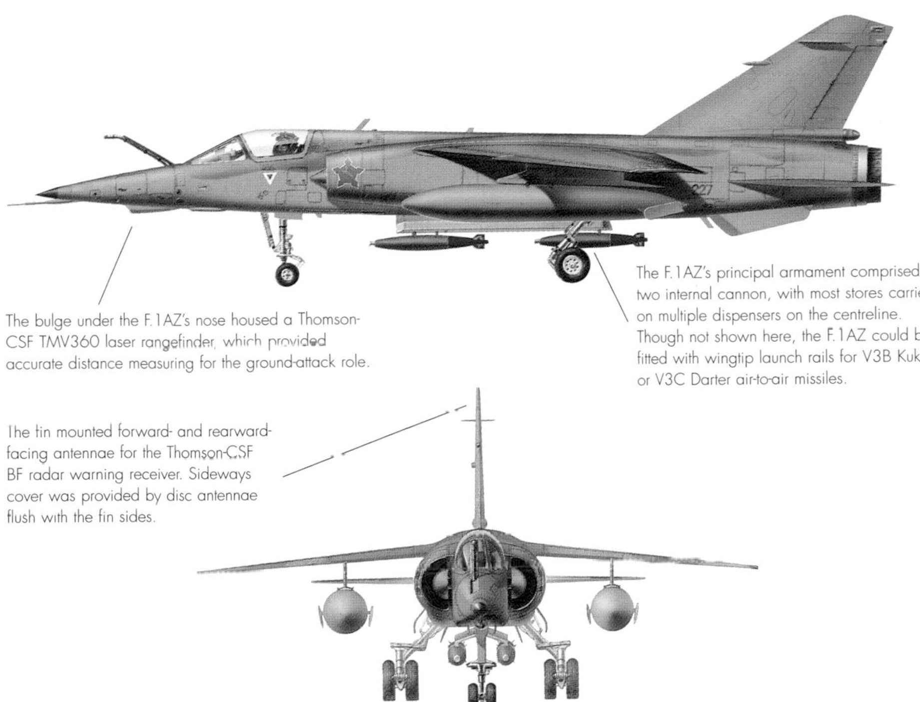

The bulge under the F.1AZ's nose housed a Thomson-CSF TMV360 laser rangefinder, which provided accurate distance measuring for the ground-attack role.

The F.1AZ's principal armament comprised two internal cannon, with most stores carried on multiple dispensers on the centreline. Though not shown here, the F.1AZ could be fitted with wingtip launch rails for V3B Kukri or V3C Darter air-to-air missiles.

The fin mounted forward- and rearward-facing antennae for the Thomson-CSF BF radar warning receiver. Sideways cover was provided by disc antennae flush with the fin sides.

This colourful Mirage F.1 was pictured at RAF Fairford, Gloucestershire.

The Mirage F.1 single-seat strike fighter was developed as a private venture. Powered by a SNECMA Atar 09K, the prototype flew for the first time on 23 December 1966; it exceeded Mach 2 in its fourth flight on 7 January 1967, but was lost in a fatal accident on 18 May that year. Development went ahead nonetheless, and the first production aircraft entered service with the 30e Escadre at Reims early in 1974. Variants produced included the F.1A ground-attack aircraft, the F.1C interceptor and the F.1B two-seat trainer. The Mirage

F.1's wing, a departure from the traditional Dassault delta format, was fitted with elaborate high-lift devices which permitted the aircraft to take off and land within 500–800m (1600–2600ft) at average combat mission weight. Primary role of the Mirage F.1 was all-weather interception at any altitude, and the original production version used the same weapon systems as the Mirage III. Large numbers of Mirage F.1s were exported overseas, notably to countries in the Middle East. These export aircraft were distinguished by a suffix letter, for example the F.1CK for Kuwait.

Dassault Mirage F.1AZ

Type:	single-seat multi-role fighter/attack aircraft
Powerplant:	one 7200kg (15,876lb) thrust SNECMA Atar 9K-50 turbojet
Performance:	maximum speed 2350km/h (1460mph) at high altitude; service ceiling 20,000m (65,615ft); range 900km (560 miles) with maximum load
Weights:	empty 7400kg (16,317lb); maximum take-off 15,200kg (33,510lb)
Dimensions:	wing span 8.40m (27ft 6.67in); length 15.0m (49ft 2.25in); height 4.50m (14ft 9in)
Armament:	two 30mm (1.19in) cannon; up to 6300kg (13,892lb) of external munitions

An F.1 joins up with a French Air Force Boeing KC-135 flight refuelling tanker.

DASSAULT SUPER ETENDARD

The Dassault Super Etendard achieved brief notoriety during the Falklands War of 1982, when aircraft armed with Exocet missiles sank the British destroyer HMS Sheffield *and the container ship* Atlantic Conveyor.

In service for over 20 years, the Super Etendard lasted far beyond its planned career, and is to be replaced by the Dassault Rafale. The example seen here belonged to the now defunct 14 Flotille, which was based at Landivisiau.

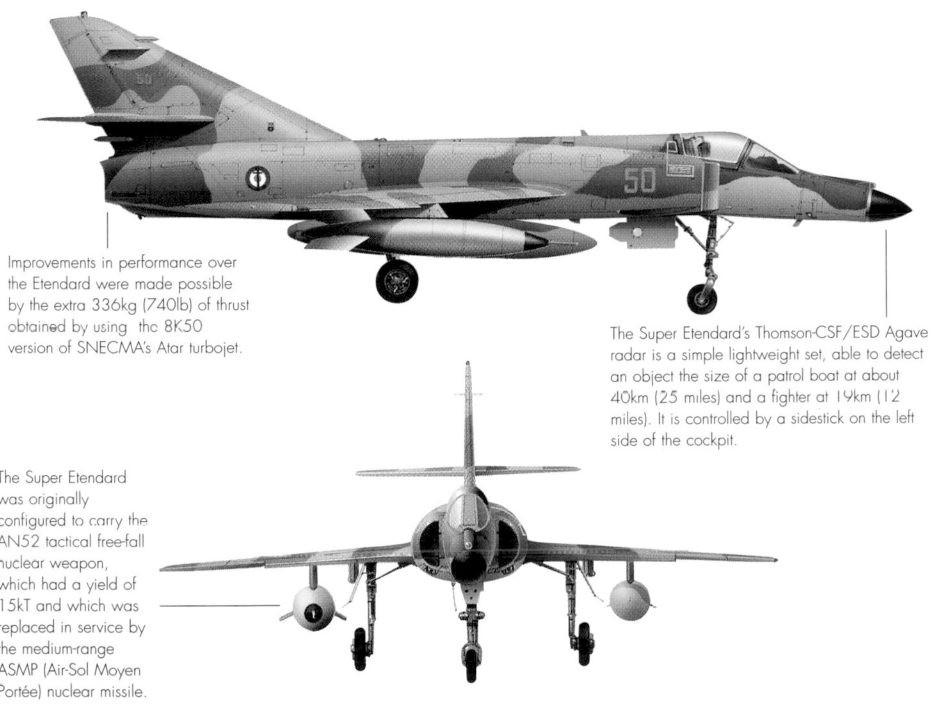

Improvements in performance over the Etendard were made possible by the extra 336kg (740lb) of thrust obtained by using the 8K50 version of SNECMA's Atar turbojet.

The Super Etendard's Thomson-CSF/ESD Agave radar is a simple lightweight set, able to detect an object the size of a patrol boat at about 40km (25 miles) and a fighter at 19km (12 miles). It is controlled by a sidestick on the left side of the cockpit.

The Super Etendard was originally configured to carry the AN52 tactical free-fall nuclear weapon, which had a yield of 15kT and which was replaced in service by the medium-range ASMP (Air-Sol Moyen Portée) nuclear missile.

Seen here is a Super Etendard taking off from a carrier, aided by the catapult.

Originally designed for a mid-1950s tactical strike fighter contest - which it lost to the Fiat G.91 - the Dassault Etendard (Standard) showed such outstanding qualities that the French Navy encouraged its development in order to meet its need for a strike aircraft capable also of high-altitude interception. The navalized prototype Etendard IVM-01 first flew on 21 May 1958. The first of 69 production Etendard IVMs was delivered to the Aéronavale on 18 January 1962, followed into service by the Etendard IVP, an unarmed reconnaissance/ tanker variant. The Super Etendard, which first flew on 3 October 1975, was fitted with a SNECMA Atar 8K-50 turbojet and was intended for the low-level attack role, primarily against shipping. Fourteen Super Etendards were supplied to Argentina from 1981, and the five that had been delivered by the time of the Falklands war of May–June 1982 proved highly effective against British vessels. French Navy Super Etendards serving on the carriers *Charles de Gaulle, Foch* and *Clemenceau* will be replaced by the Dassault Rafale by 2010.

Dassault Super Etendard

Type:	single-seat carrier-borne strike and interceptor aircraft
Powerplant:	one 5000kg (11025lb) thrust SNECMA Atar 8K-50 turbojet
Performance:	maximum speed 1180km/h (733mph) at low level; service ceiling 13,700m (44,947ft); combat radius 850km (528 miles)
Weights:	empty 6500kg (14,333lb); maximum take-off 12,000kg (26,455lb)
Dimensions:	wing span 9.60m (31ft 6in); length 14.31m (46ft 11in); height 3.86m (12ft 8in)
Armament:	two 30mm (1.19in) cannon; provision for up to 2100kg (4630lb) of external munitions

The 1982 Falklands war highlighted the Super Etendard's impressive capabilities.

FRANCE

DASSAULT MIRAGE 2000C

One of aviation's great success stories has been France's Dassault Mirage family, one of the most versatile of which is the multi-role Mirage 2000.

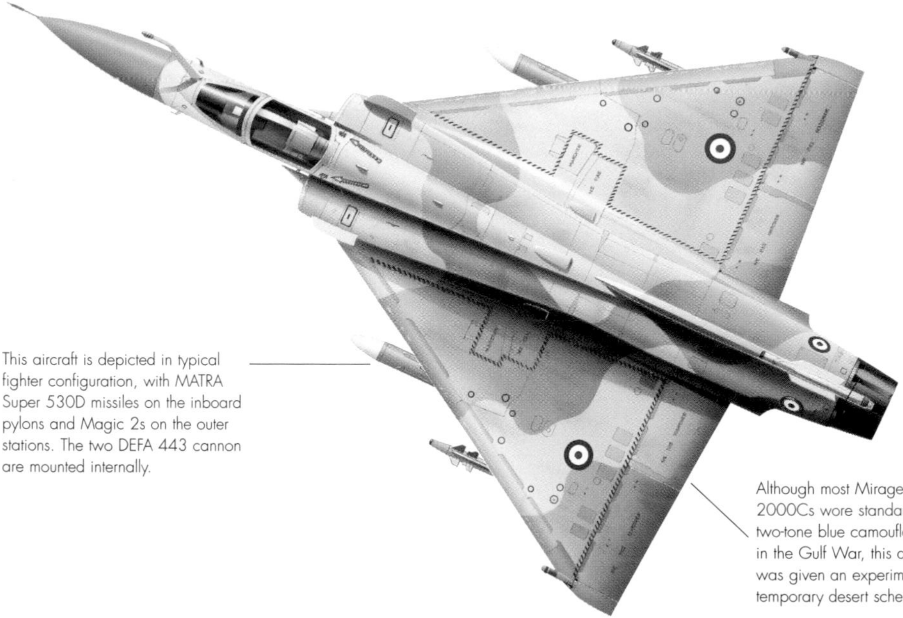

This aircraft is depicted in typical fighter configuration, with MATRA Super 530D missiles on the inboard pylons and Magic 2s on the outer stations. The two DEFA 443 cannon are mounted internally.

Although most Mirage 2000Cs wore standard two-tone blue camouflage in the Gulf War, this aircraft was given an experimental temporary desert scheme.

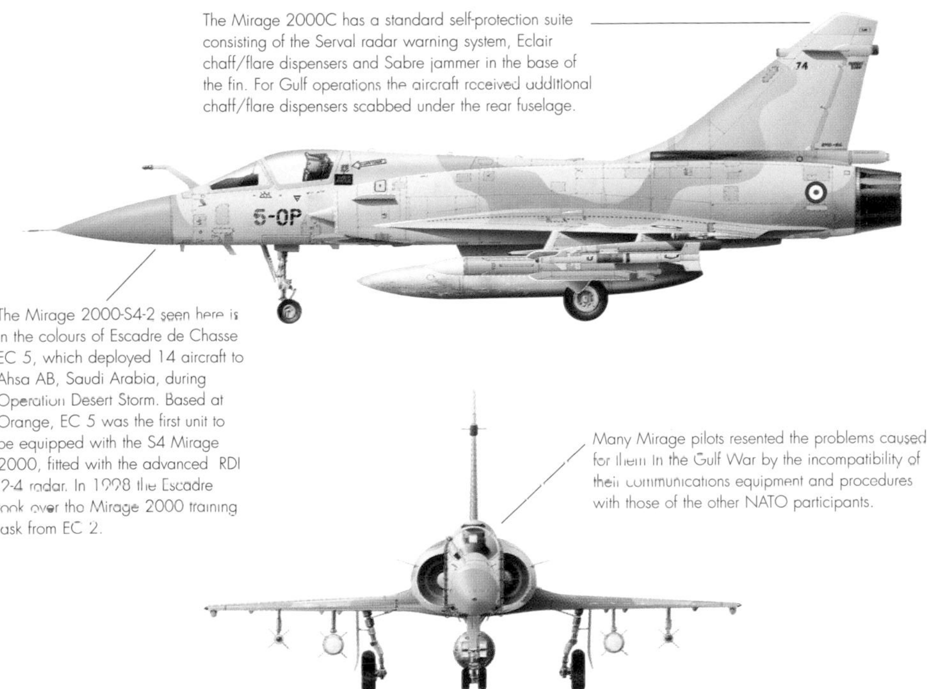

The Mirage 2000C has a standard self-protection suite consisting of the Serval radar warning system, Eclair chaff/flare dispensers and Sabre jammer in the base of the fin. For Gulf operations the aircraft received additional chaff/flare dispensers scabbed under the rear fuselage.

The Mirage 2000-S4-2 seen here is in the colours of Escadre de Chasse EC 5, which deployed 14 aircraft to Ahsa AB, Saudi Arabia, during Operation Desert Storm. Based at Orange, EC 5 was the first unit to be equipped with the S4 Mirage 2000, fitted with the advanced RDI J2-4 radar. In 1998 the Escadre took over the Mirage 2000 training task from EC 2.

Many Mirage pilots resented the problems caused for them in the Gulf War by the incompatibility of their communications equipment and procedures with those of the other NATO participants.

This Mirage 2000C displays the air-to-air armament of its four wing pylons.

The Mirage 2000, the first of the Mirage family to take advantage of 'fly-by-wire' technology, was designed as an interceptor to replace the Mirage F.1. Its development began after the failure of various programmes including the Anglo-French Variable Geometry Aircraft, and the ACF (Avion de Combat Futur/Future Combat Aircraft). The Mirage 2000 was formally adopted instead by the French government on 18 December 1975 as the primary French Air Force combat aircraft from the mid-1980s. Five prototypes were built, the first flying on

10 March 1978. A two-seat version, the Mirage 2000B (the fifth prototype) flew on 11 October 1980. The first unit to become operational with the Mirage 2000C-1 was the elite Escadre de Chasse 1/2 'Cigognes' at Dijon (on 2 July 1984). The Mirage 2000N, first flown on 2 February 1983, was developed as a replacement for the Mirage IIIE and is armed with the ASMP medium-range nuclear missile. Like its predecessors, the Mirage 2000 has been exported in large numbers to Abu Dhabi, Egypt, Greece, India and Peru. In Indian Air Force service the aircraft, designated Mirage 2000H, is known as the Vajra (Thunderstreak).

Dassault Mirage 2000C

Type:	single-seat air superiority and attack fighter
Powerplant:	one 9700kg (21,389lb) thrust SNECMA M53-P2 turbofan
Performance:	maximum speed 2338km/h (1453mph); service ceiling 18,000m (59,055ft); range 1480km (920 miles)
Weights:	empty 7500kg (16,538lb); maximum take-off 17,000kg (37,485lb)
Dimensions:	wing span 9.13m (29ft 11.5in); length 14.36m (47ft 1.25in); height 5.20m (17ft 0.67in)
Armament:	two 30mm (1.18in) cannon; up to 6300kg (13,892lb) of external munitions

A Mirage 2000C taxies round the perimeter track of a French airfield.

Aeritalia G.91

In the 1950s, NATO air commanders were keen to develop a lightweight tactical jet fighter-bomber that could operate from makeshift airstrips if conventional runways were destroyed. The result was the G.91.

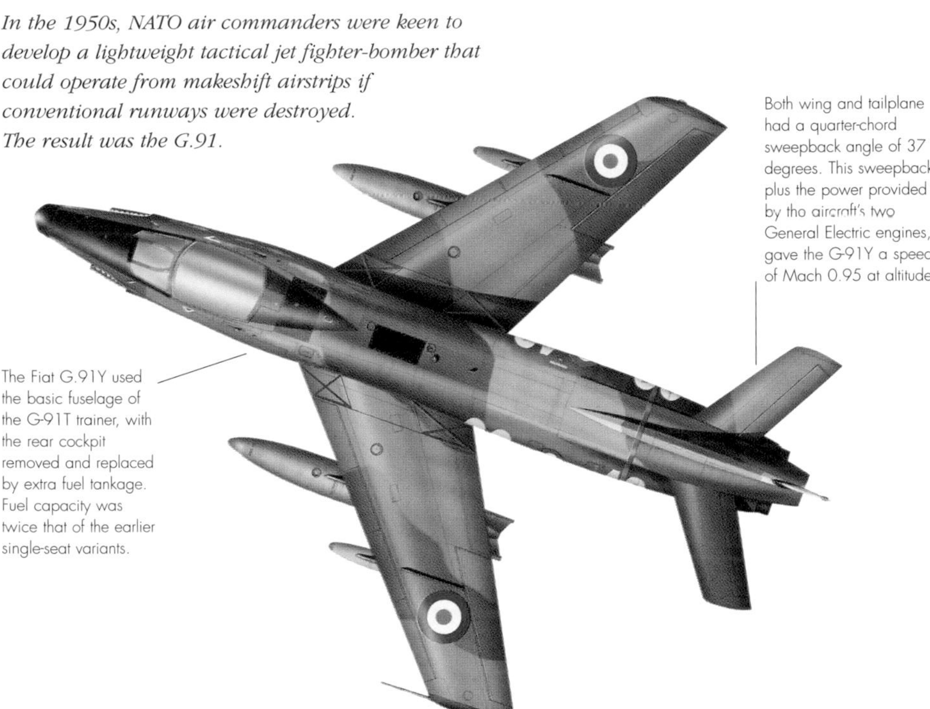

Both wing and tailplane had a quarter-chord sweepback angle of 37 degrees. This sweepback, plus the power provided by the aircraft's two General Electric engines, gave the G-91Y a speed of Mach 0.95 at altitude.

The Fiat G.91Y used the basic fuselage of the G-91T trainer, with the rear cockpit removed and replaced by extra fuel tankage. Fuel capacity was twice that of the earlier single-seat variants.

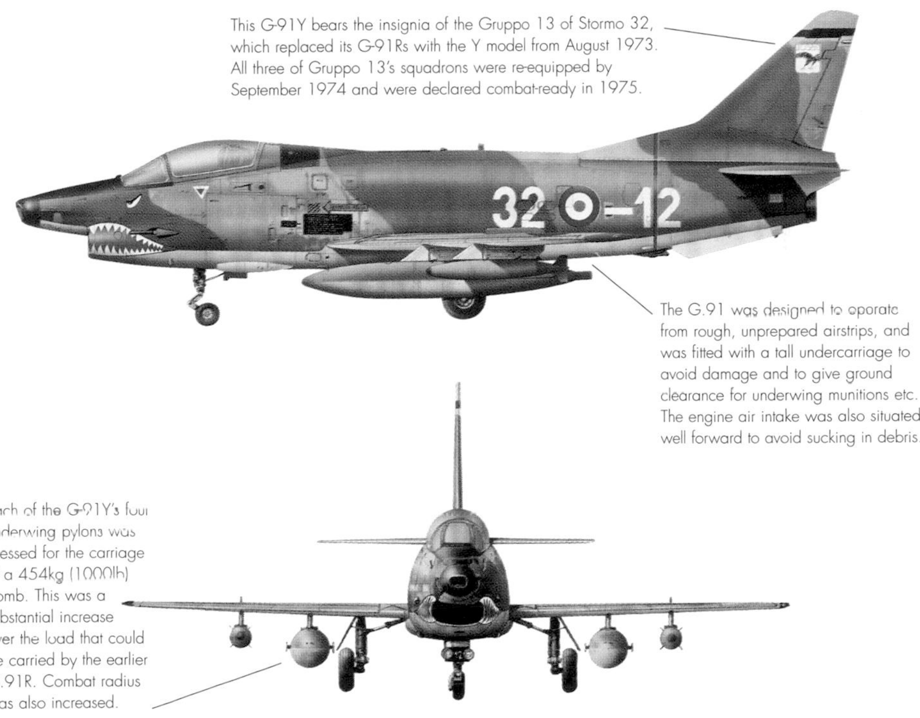

This G-91Y bears the insignia of the Gruppo 13 of Stormo 32, which replaced its G-91Rs with the Y model from August 1973. All three of Gruppo 13's squadrons were re-equipped by September 1974 and were declared combat-ready in 1975.

The G.91 was designed to operate from rough, unprepared airstrips, and was fitted with a tall undercarriage to avoid damage and to give ground clearance for underwing munitions etc. The engine air intake was also situated well forward to avoid sucking in debris.

Each of the G-91Y's four underwing pylons was stressed for the carriage of a 454kg (1000lb) bomb. This was a substantial increase over the load that could be carried by the earlier G.91R. Combat radius was also increased.

Produced by Fiat, the Aeritalia G.91 lightweight ground-attack fighter was designed in response to a NATO requirement issued in 1954. The first prototype flew on 9 August 1956 and proved easily capable of meeting all the demands of the NATO specification. Total production of all G.91 variants from 1956 to 1977 was 756. The initial version, the G.91R, was supplied to the Italian Air Force (90) and the Federal German Luftwaffe (50 built in Italy and 294 in Germany). 50 more, originally intended for Turkey and Greece,

An Aeritalia G-91R, used here as a tactical reconnaissance aircraft.

were eventually delivered to Germany. The second basic version was the G.91T two-seat trainer, 99 being built for Italy and 66 for Germany. The last G.91 variant was the G.91Y, which was substantially redesigned and had two General Electric J85 turbojets to allow a greater tactical load. The prototype flew on 27 December 1966 and was followed by 20 pre-series and 45 production aircraft for the Italian Air Force.

Aeritalia G-91Y

Type:	single-seat tactical reconnaissance aircraft
Powerplant:	two General Electric J85-GE-13A turbojets, each delivering 1235kg (2723lb) thrust
Performance:	maximum speed 1110km/h (690mph); service ceiling 12,500m (41,000ft); combat radius 750km (466 miles)
Weights:	empty 3900kg (8600lb); maximum take-off 8700kg (19,184lb)
Dimensions:	wing span 9.01m (29ft 6.5in); length 11.67m (38ft 3.5in); height 4.43m (14ft 6in)
Armament:	two 30mm (1.19in) cannon; four pylons for various ordnance; three camera installations

The G.91 was widely used by both the Italian Air Force and the Luftwaffe.

INTERNATIONAL

AMX

The AMX tactical support aircraft, developed jointly by Italy and Brazil, follows the trend of international co-operation established by the European nations.

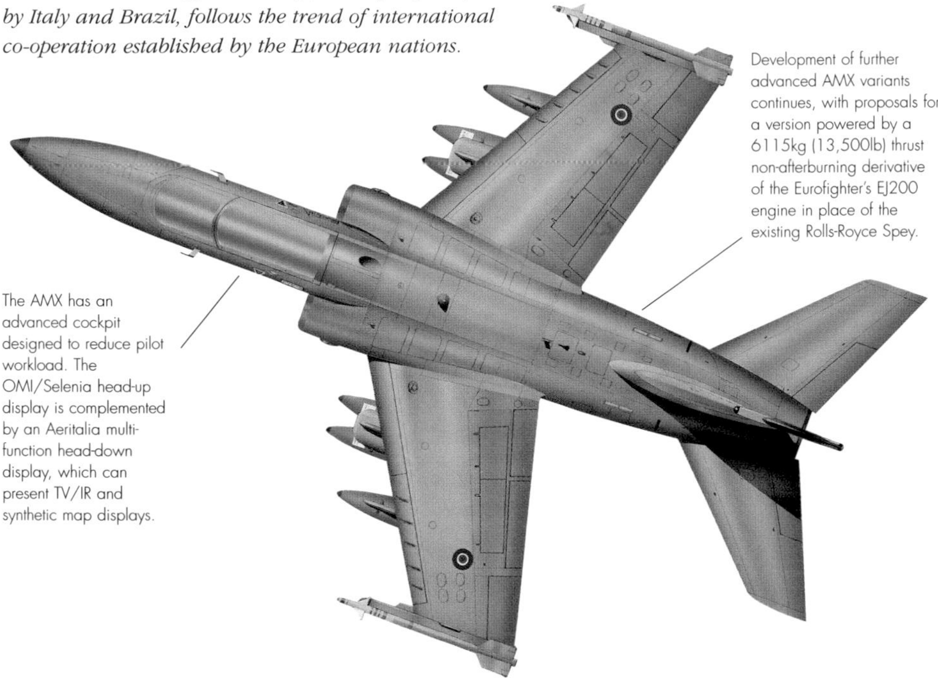

Development of further advanced AMX variants continues, with proposals for a version powered by a 6115kg (13,500lb) thrust non-afterburning derivative of the Eurofighter's EJ200 engine in place of the existing Rolls-Royce Spey.

The AMX has an advanced cockpit designed to reduce pilot workload. The OMI/Selenia head-up display is complemented by an Aeritalia multi-function head-down display, which can present TV/IR and synthetic map displays.

Italian AMXs have a simple I-band ranging radar, the FIAR-built version of the Israeli ELTA EL/M-2001B. Brazilian aircraft have a similar radar, the Technasa/SMA SCP-01.

The 51 nose code and the cat and mouse fin badge identify this aircraft as one of those delivered to the first operational AMX unit: Gruppo 103, Stormo 51, based at Istrana. The unit was previously equipped with the Fiat G-91R.

The AMX is cleared to use a wide variety of weapons, including free-fall and retarded Mk 82, Mk 83, Mk 84 bombs and the Skyshark munitions dispenser system. Sidewinder or Piranha AAMs can be carried for self-defence.

The AMX was the product of collaboration between the Italian companies Alenia and Aermacchi on the one hand, and the Brazilian Embraer company on the other, and was the result of a joint requirement formulated by both countries for a new lightweight tactical fighter-bomber. The selected powerplant was the Rolls-Royce Spey turbofan, built under licence by an Italian consortium. The first prototype flew in May 1984. The aircraft entered service with the Italian Air Force in 1990, and deliveries to the Brazilian

An AMX-ATA (Advanced Trainer and Attack) version of the basic AMX.

Air Force began a year later. The AMX-T is a two-seat, high performance trainer version, and has been selected by the Venezuelan Air Force to replace its T-2A Buckeyes in the advanced training role. The AMX is capable of operating at high subsonic speed and low altitude, by day or night, and if necessary from bases with poorly maintained or damaged runways. It has a low infrared signature, reduced radar equivalent cross section, and low vulnerability of structure and systems.

AMX

Type:	single-seat multi-role combat aircraft
Powerplant:	one 5003kg (11,032lb) thrust Rolls-Royce Spey Mk 807/8 turbofan
Performance:	maximum speed 1047km/h (651mph); service ceiling 13,000m (42,650ft); combat radius 556km (345 miles)
Weights:	empty 6631kg (14,618lb); maximum take-off 13,000kg (28,660lb)
Dimensions:	wing span 8.87m (29ft 1.5in); length 13.23m (43ft 5in); height 4.55m (14ft 11in)
Armament:	one 20mm (0.79in) or two 30mm (1.19in) cannon (Brazilian aircraft); five hardpoints for up to 3800kg (8377lb) of ordnance; 2AAMs

The AMX programme was of vital importance to Italy's aircraft industry.

DASSAULT/DORNIER ALPHA JET

In 1968, France and Germany, both of whom had projects for an advanced jet trainer under study, decided to pool their resources and expertise. The result was the excellent Alpha Jet.

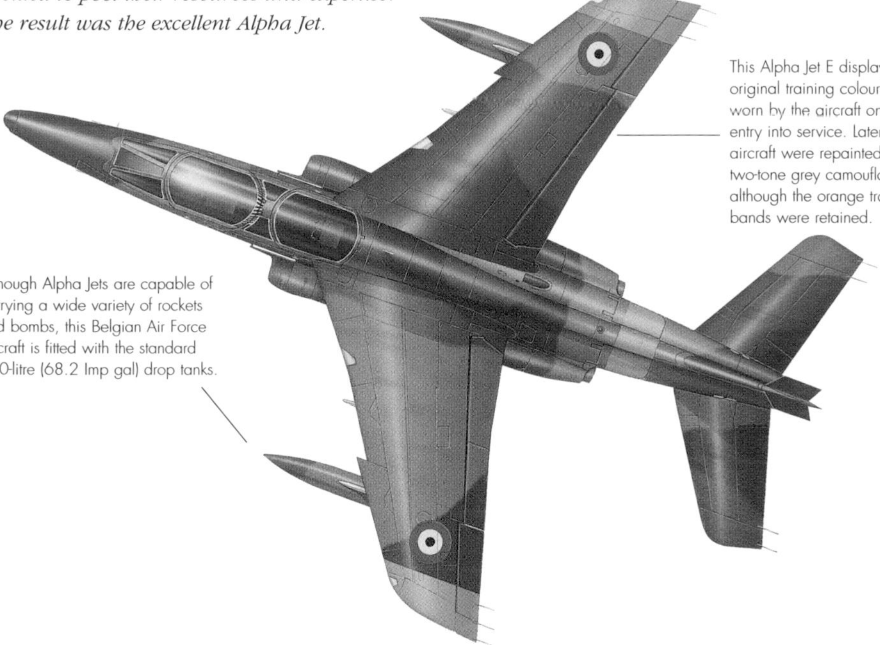

This Alpha Jet E displays the original training colours worn by the aircraft on their entry into service. Later, the aircraft were repainted in a two-tone grey camouflage, although the orange training bands were retained.

Although Alpha Jets are capable of carrying a wide variety of rockets and bombs, this Belgian Air Force aircraft is fitted with the standard 310-litre (68.2 Imp gal) drop tanks.

The two crew members are accommodated in tandem under individual transparencies on Martin-Baker Mk 10 ejection seats, the forward pilot being provided with a simplified head-up display. Instruments are duplicated in front and rear cockpits.

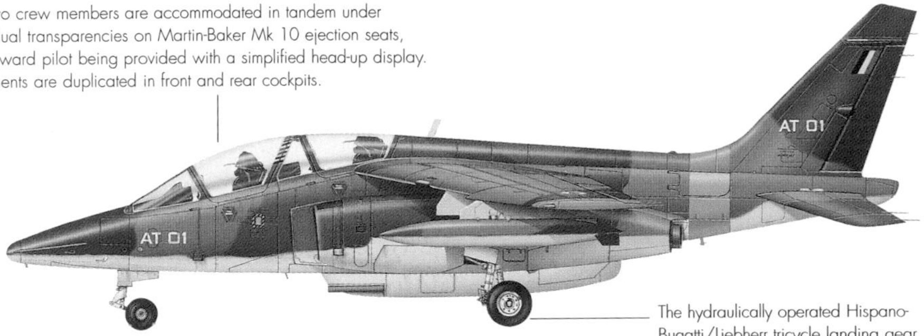

The hydraulically operated Hispano-Bugatti/Liebherr tricycle landing gear features low-pressure tyres (on main wheels only) and anti-skid brakes.

The SNECMA/Turbomeca Larzac 04-C6, two of which are installed in the Alpha Jet in nacelles on the fuselage sides, is a turbofan of 1.13 bypass ratio with a two-stage fan, four-stage HP compressor, single-stage HP turbine (having cooled blades) and single-stage LP turbine.

A French Alpha Jet E, widely used as a basic and advanced jet trainer.

Early in the joint development programme the Germans decided they did not need a training version of the Alpha Jet, but a need was identified for a light attack aircraft to replace the Fiat G-91R. In February 1972 two prototypes each were ordered by France and Germany, and the French-built version flew for the first time on 26 October 1973. Production began some time later, the first trials aircraft being delivered to the French Air Force late in 1977. Re-equipment of French training units started in May 1979, the

Alpha Jets replacing the Lockeed-Canadair T-33 and, at a later date, the Mystere IVA single-seat weapons training aircraft. The two principal versions were Alpha Jet A (A for Appui, or support) light attack aircraft, and the Alpha Jet E (E for Ecole, or School) basic and advanced trainer. The E model, which also has a light attack capability, was produced for the French Air Force and a number of foreign customers, while deliveries of the A model to the Federal German Luftwaffe began in 1979 (175 were delivered between then and 1983). The French Air Force took delivery of 176 aircraft between 1978 and 1985, and export customers include Belgium, Cameroon, Côte d'Ivoire, Egypt, Morocco, Portugal, Qatar and Togo.

Dassault/Dornier Alpha Jet E

Type:	two-seat basic/advanced trainer
Powerplant:	two 1350kg (2977lb) Turbomeca Larzac 04 turbofans
Performance:	maximum speed 927km/h (576mph); service ceiling 14,000m (45,930ft); low-level mission range 583km (363 miles)
Weights:	empty 3345kg (7376lb); maximum take-off 8000kg (17,640lb)
Dimensions:	wing span 9.11m (29ft 10.67in); length 13.23m (43ft 5in); height 4.19m (13ft 9in)
Armament:	one 30mm (1.19in) cannon (optional)

A Luftwaffe Alpha Jet A. Note the 27mm (1.06in) IWKA Mauser cannon pod.

INTERNATIONAL

A Royal Navy Merlin in flight over the Type 23 frigate HMS *Norfolk*.

The EH101 helicopter was developed jointly by Britain's GKN-Westland Helicopters and Italy's Agusta for both civil and military applications. The programme was given the go-ahead by the British and Italian governments with the signing of an agreement on 25 January 1984. This provided for joint funding of the project through development and production. The EH101 subsequently entered full production in both Italy and the United Kingdom, with orders placed by the Royal Navy (Merlin HM Mk 1) and Royal

Air Force (Merlin HC.Mk.3), the Italian Navy, the Canadian Armed Forces, the Danish armed forces and the Tokyo Police. The Merlin Mk 3, pioneered into RAF service by No 28 Squadron, is the first helicopter to enter service with an integrated Defensive Aids Suite (DAS), giving the highest level of self-protection of any UK military helicopter. The enhancement consists of an infrared countermeasures system incorporating a passive missile warning system (MWS). The EH101's roles include tactical troop transport, search and rescue, combat search and rescue and anti-submarine warfare.

EH101 Merlin HM.Mk.I

Type	ASW/general-purpose helicopter with three crew
Powerplant:	three Rolls-Royce/Turbomeca RTM-322 turbines
Performance:	maximum speed 280km/h (174mph); service ceiling 4575m (15,000ft); range 1389km (863 miles)
Weights:	empty 8600kg (18,963lb); maximum take-off 14,600kg (32,188lb)
Dimensions:	main rotor diameter 18.6m (61ft); fuselage length 19.63m (64ft 5in); height 6.63m (21ft 9in)
Armament:	variety of ASW and anti-shipping munitions, sonobuoys etc

A Merlin carrying out trials with the Type 23 frigate HMS *Iron Duke* in 1992.

INTERNATIONAL

DA 7, one of the development Eurofighters, in Italian markings.

The Eurofighter is based on the agile demonstrator aircraft created under the Experimental Aircraft Programme, or EAP. This flew for the first time on 8 August 1986, and was the most advanced aircraft ever produced in Britain. The weapons chosen for Eurofighter are the Hughes AIM-120 AMRAAM as the primary weapon, with the AIM-132 ASRAAM as the secondary. The aircraft also has a built-in gun armament. A major asset is the pilot's head-mounted sight, avoiding the need to pull tight turns to achieve missile lock-on.

The first two Eurofighter prototypes flew in 1994, followed by several more. The original customer requirement was 250 each for the UK and Germany, 165 for Italy and 100 for Spain. Spain announced a firm requirement for 87 in January 1994, while Germany and Italy revised their respective needs to 180 and 121, the German order to include at least 40 examples of the fighter-bomber version. The UK's order was 232, with options on a further 65. Deliveries to the air forces of all four countries were scheduled to begin in 2001, although this schedule has slipped. Austria has announced it will buy 35 Eurofighters.

Eurofighter Typhoon

Type:	single-seat multi-role combat aircraft
Powerplant:	two 9185kg (20,253lb) thrust Eurojet EJ.200 turbofans
Performance:	maximum speed 2125km/h (1321 mph) at 11,000m (36,090ft); service ceiling classified; range classified
Weights:	empty 9750kg (21,499lb); maximum take-off 21,000kg (46,305lb)
Dimensions:	wing span 10.5m (34ft 5.5in); length 14.50m (47ft 7in); height 4.0m (13ft 1.5in)
Armament:	one 23mm (0.906in) cannon; 13 hardpoints for a variety of ordnance including AMRAAM, ASRAAM, ASMs, anti-radar missiles, guided and unguided bombs

Eurofighter Development Aircraft DA 5, based at Daimler-Benz Aerospace AG.

SEPECAT JAGUAR

Designed as a tactical support aircraft, the Anglo-French Jaguar saw action during the Gulf War of 1991 and proved its worth beyond all doubt in precision attacks on Iraqi positions.

The Jaguar can carry a maximum warload of eight 454kg (1000lb) bombs, but four was a more typical load on Gulf War missions. This example is carrying two laser-guided bombs, with Sidewinders on overwing mounts for self-defence. An MTRA Phimat chaff-dispensing pod is under the starboard wing, and an AN/ALQ-101 jammer is on the port outer pylon.

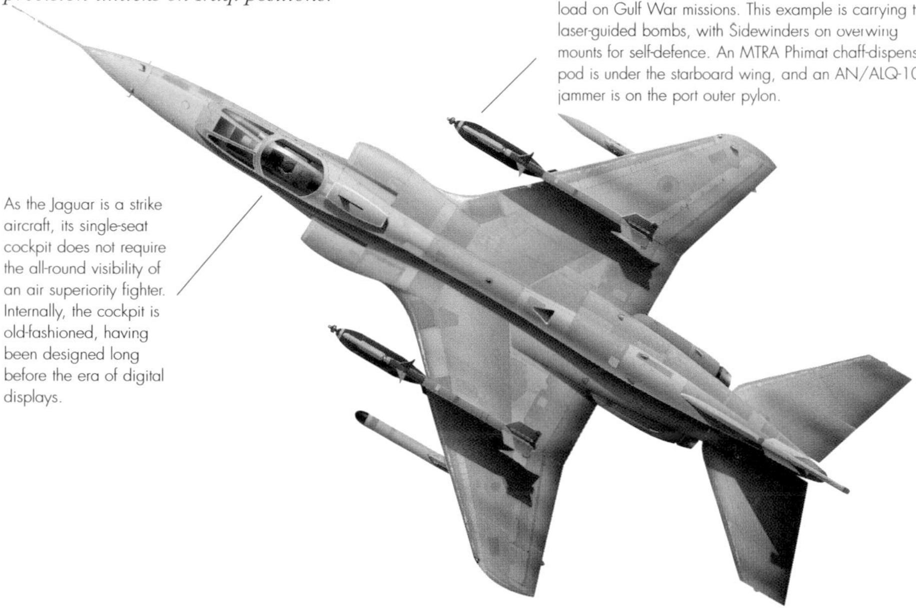

As the Jaguar is a strike aircraft, its single-seat cockpit does not require the all-round visibility of an air superiority fighter. Internally, the cockpit is old-fashioned, having been designed long before the era of digital displays.

This Jaguar GR.1A, XZ364 'Sadman' of the Coltishall Wing, deployed to Muharraq in Bahrain for combat operations during Operation Desert Storm, in which it flew 47 sorties. Note the desert camouflage and the nose art, which depicts Saddam Hussein ('Sadman Insane') on the receiving end of a British boot.

The characteristic wedge or 'chisel' shape of the Jaguar's nose encloses the aircraft's Ferranti laser rangefinder and marked target seeker.

A hard-hitting 30mm (1.19in) ADEN Mk.4 cannon is mounted on either side of the fuselage, below the engine air intakes. Each gun carries 150 rounds. Jaguars made highly successful cannon attacks against Iraqi naval patrol vessels that were trying to flee to safety and internment in neighbouring Iran.

Developed jointly by the British Aircraft Corporation and Breguet (later Dassault-Breguet) under the banner of SEPECAT, the Jaguar emerged from protracted development as a much more powerful and effective aircraft than originally envisaged. The first French version to fly, in September 1968, was the two-seat E model, 40 being ordered by the French Air Force, followed in March 1969 by the single-seat Jaguar A tactical support aircraft. Service deliveries of the E began in May 1972, the first of 160 Jaguar As

Two Jaguar GR.1s of No 20 Squadron RAF, armed with laser-guided bombs.

following in 1973. The British versions, known as the Jaguar S (strike) and Jaguar B (trainer), flew on 12 October 1969 and 30 August 1971 respectively, being delivered to the RAF as the Jaguar GR.Mk.1 (165 examples) and Jaguar T.Mk.2/2A (38). The Jaguar GR.1A/3A are upgrades. The Jaguar International, first flown in August 1976, was a version developed for the export market. It was purchased by Ecuador (12), Nigeria (18) and Oman (24) and was licence-built in India by HAL (98, including 40 delivered by B.Ae). A French plan to produce a carrier-borne version of the Jaguar was abandoned, the Dassault Super Etendard being ordered instead.

SEPECAT Jaguar GR.Mk.1A

Type:	single-seat tactical support and strike aircraft
Powerplant:	two 3313kg (7305lb) thrust Rolls-Royce/Turbomeca Adour Mk 102 turbofans
Performance:	maximum speed 1593km/h (990mph) at 11,000m (36,090ft); service ceiling 15,240m (50,000ft); combat range 557km (346 miles)
Weights:	empty 7000kg (15,435lb); maximum take-off 15,500kg (34,178lb)
Dimensions:	wing span 8.69m (28ft 6in); length 16.83m (55ft 2.5in); height: 4.89m (16ft 0.5in)
Armament:	two 30mm (1.19in) cannon; five external hardpoints for 4536kg (10,000lb) of munitions; two AAMs

Note the Sidewinder AAMs on their overwing stations on this RAF Jaguar.

The first version of the Tornado ADV was the F.2, seen here on a test flight.

Three Tornado ADV prototypes were built, all powered by the Turbo-Union RB199 Mk103 turbofan, which was also to power the initial production batch of Tornado F.2s for the RAF. These aircraft also had manually swept wings (automatic on later production aircraft). Armament trials were carried out with development aircraft 02, including Sky Flash AAM firings and Mauser gun firing trials. Early problems with the AI.24 Foxhunter radar were still far from resolved when the first Tornado F.2s were delivered to No 229 Operational

Conversion Unit (OCU) at RAF Coningsby, in Lincolnshire, in November 1984. The first eighteen aircraft were all powered by Mk103 engines; aircraft after that had the more powerful Mk104 and these were designated F.3. The first F.3 squadron, No 29, formed at RAF Coningsby in May 1987 and was declared operational at the end of November. The aircraft eventually armed seven squadrons in addition to No 229 OCU (which became No 56 Reserve Squadron on 1 July 1992). The Tornado ADV also serves with the air forces of Italy and Saudi Arabia.

Panavia Tornado ADV

Type:	two-seat all-weather air defence aircraft
Powerplant:	two 7290kg (16,075lb) thrust Turbo-Union RB.199-34R Mk 104 turbofans
Performance:	maximum speed 2337km/h (1452mph); service ceiling 21,335m (70,000ft);
Weights:	empty 14,501kg (31,979lb); maximum take-off 27,987kg (61,700lb)
Dimensions:	wing span 13.91m (45ft 7.67in) spread and 8.6m (28ft 2.5in) swept; length 18.68m (61ft 3in); height 5.95m (19ft 6.25in)
Armament:	two 27mm (1.063in) cannon; up to 5806kg (12,800lb) of AAMs

This prototype F.2 is carrying four dummy Skyflash air-to-air missiles.

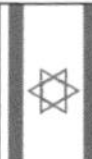

ISRAELI AIRCRAFT INDUSTRIES KFIR

Sometimes, nations which rely on foreign imports to meet their combat aircraft needs find themselves faced with a crisis which compels them to fall back on their own resources. That was how the IAI Kfir originated.

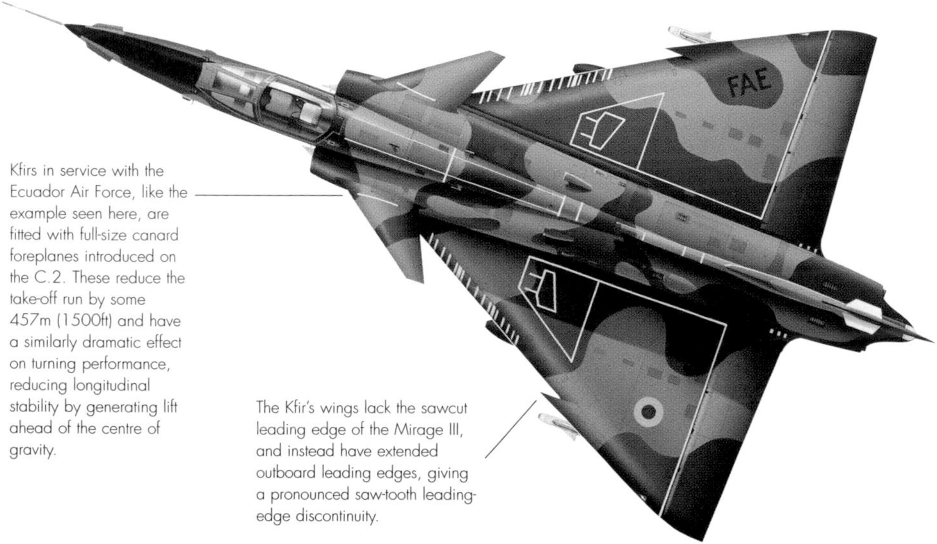

Kfirs in service with the Ecuador Air Force, like the example seen here, are fitted with full-size canard foreplanes introduced on the C.2. These reduce the take-off run by some 457m (1500ft) and have a similarly dramatic effect on turning performance, reducing longitudinal stability by generating lift ahead of the centre of gravity.

The Kfir's wings lack the sawcut leading edge of the Mirage III, and instead have extended outboard leading edges, giving a pronounced saw-tooth leading-edge discontinuity.

The Kfir was powered by the most powerful production variant of the General Electric J79 engine, the J79-J1E. Because it had greater mass flow than the original Mirage III Atar engine, installation of the J79 necessitated larger intakes, and its increased operating temperatures required the provision of a dorsal airscoop.

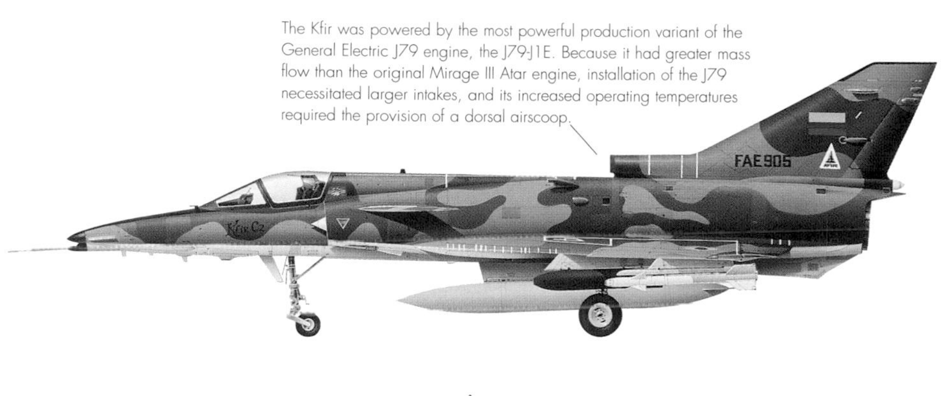

The Kfir C.2 carries a fixed armament of two 30mm (1.19in) DEFA 553 cannon just ahead of the wing roots, each with 125 rounds of ammunition. The aircraft also carries two Rafael Shafrir air-to-air infra red homing missiles.

Three Mitsubishi F.1s seen flying in close formation during an exercise.

The second and third production T-2s were converted as prototypes, and the first of 77 F-1s was delivered in September 1977 to the 3rd Hikotai (Squadron) at Misawa. This unit transferred to the control of the 3rd Kokudan (Wing) on 1 March 1978 when conversion was complete. The 3rd Kokudan's second squadron, the 8th Hikotai, began conversion to the F-1 on 30 June 1979, and when this was complete the 6th Hikotai began their transfer to the new aircraft on 11 March 1980. Squadrons originally formed with 18 aircraft each (plus replacements) but this was felt to be too small a number, and the JASDF pushed hard for an increase in unit establishment. The Japanese Defence Ministry responded by threatening to reduce the number of F-1 squadrons to two, and the JASDF gave in. The last F-1 delivery was made in March 1987, and by 2000 the last 60 or so surviving aircraft equipped two squadrons, which were awaiting the arrival of the F-1's replacement, the Mitsubishi F-2, a much-modified derivative of the Lockheed Martin F-16.

Mitsubishi F-1

Type:	single-seat strike fighter
Powerplant:	two 3315kg (7308lb) thrust Ishikawajima-Harima TF40 IHI-801A turbojets
Performance:	maximum speed 1708km/h (1061mph) at 10,675m (35,000ft); service ceiling 15,240m (50,000ft); combat radius 350km (218 miles)
Weights:	empty 6358kg (14,017lb); maximum take-off 13,700kg (30,203lb)
Dimensions:	wing span 7.88m (25ft 10in); length 17.86m (58ft 7in); height 4.39m (14ft 4.67in)
Armament:	one 20mm (0.79in) six barrel cannon; five hardpoints for up to 2722kg (6000lb) of munitions

From most angles the F-1 bears a strong resemblance to the SEPECAT Jaguar.

JAPAN

JAPAN

Shin Meiwa US-1A

As an island nation, Japan has an ongoing requirement for maritime search and rescue facilities. In recent years, one of its best assets in this respect has been the US-1 long-range seaplane.

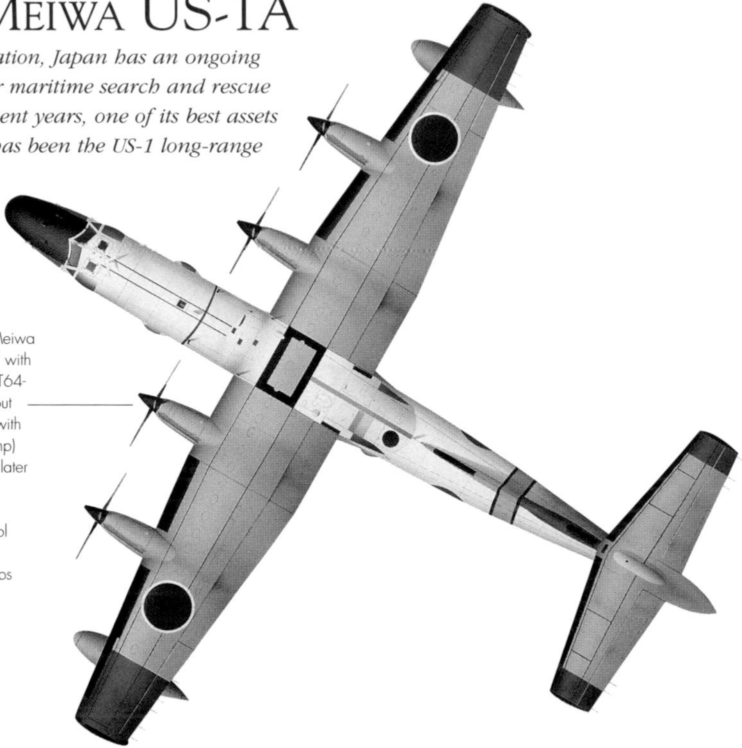

The first seven Shin Meiwa US-1s were delivered with 2282kW (3060hp) T64-IHI-10E turboprops, but were later retrofitted with the 2602kW (3490hp) 10J engines used on later aircraft. An auxiliary engine powered the boundary layer control system, blowing high pressure air to the flaps and tail surfaces.

The Shin Meiwa US-1 could carry up to 20 seated survivors and 12 stretcher cases in its standard fit, although alternative configurations allowed greater numbers to be carried. Inflatable rubber life rafts were launched through the large fuselage access door.

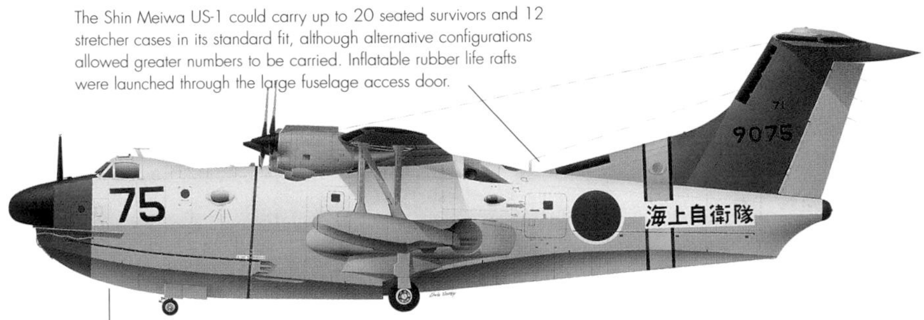

The original PS-1 ASW flying boat served with the 31st Kokutai from 1971 until 1989, when the aircraft was retired. Plans for a second unit, the 32nd Kokutai, were abandoned. The SAR-configured US-1 served with the 71st Kokutai at Iwakuni.

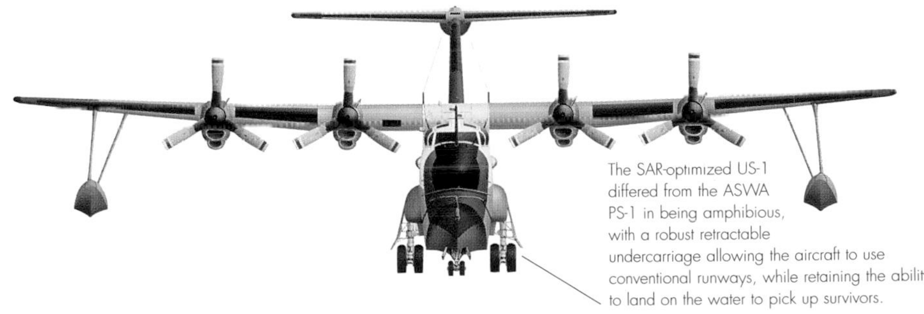

The SAR-optimized US-1 differed from the ASWA PS-1 in being amphibious, with a robust retractable undercarriage allowing the aircraft to use conventional runways, while retaining the ability to land on the water to pick up survivors.

A Shin Meiwa PS-1 anti-submarine patrol aircraft off the Japanese coast.

First flown on 5 October 1967 as the PX-S, this long-range STOL amphibious seaplane entered service with the Japanese forces in 1973 in its PS-1 anti-submarine form. The aircraft had been completely retired by 1989, but early in PS-1 production Shin Meiwa were asked to develop an amphibious version for search and rescue (SAR) duties. This emerged as the US-1, which flew in prototype form on 15 October 1974. The US-1 was virtually identical to the PS-1, but with the exception of ocean search radar all sensor systems were deleted, as was the armament. Additional 'bubble' windows were provided for observers, and along with rescue hatches with folding ramps, a large sliding door was built into the starboard side of the aircraft to allow launch and recovery of an inflatable rescue dinghy. A batch of 12 US-1s was built, followed by two more, the 7th and subsequent aircraft having uprated engines and being designated US-1A. The US-1 was heavily involved in SAR activities following the shooting down of Korean Air Lines Flight 007 by the Russians in 1983.

Shin Meiwa US-1A

Type:	search and rescue amphibious seaplane with 9 crew
Powerplant:	four 2602kW (3490hp) Ishikawajima-built General Electric T64-1H1-10J turboprops
Performance:	maximum speed 495km/h (310mph) at 1500m (5000ft); service ceiling 8200m (27,000ft); range 4200km (2610 miles)
Weights:	empty 25,500kg (56228lb); maximum take off 45,000kg (99,225lb)
Dimensions:	wing span 33.15m (108ft 9in); length 33.46m (109ft 9in); height 9.82m (32ft 3in)
Armament:	none

This PS-1 was modified as a water bomber for dealing with forest fires.

JAPAN

ATLAS CHEETAH

For many years the South African Air Force relied on two principal sources – France and Israel – for its combat aircraft. Then a UN arms embargo forced South Africa to develop its own: the Cheetah.

The Cheetah C uses a new two-tone grey camouflage scheme with a large, darker diamond-shaped panel to obscure the shape of the delta wing in flight. The SAAF markings on the wings are also toned down until they are barely visible.

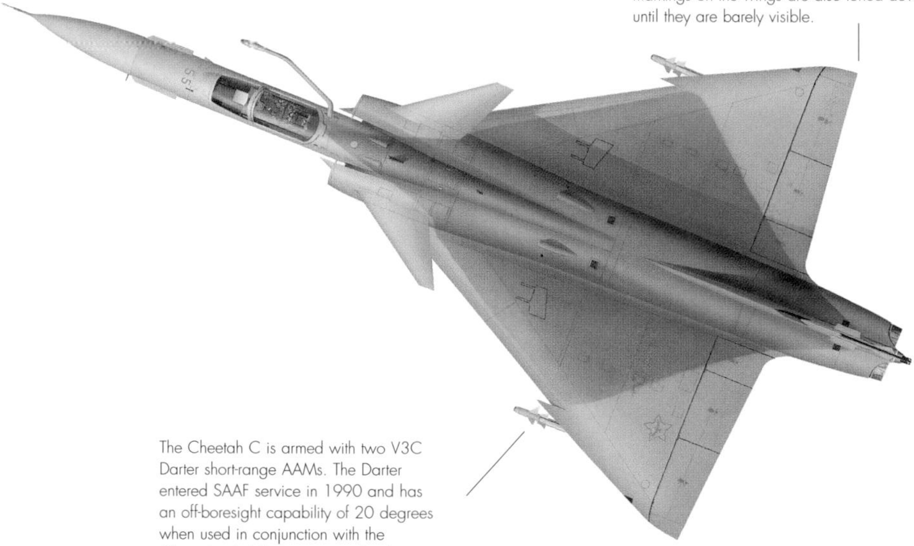

The Cheetah C is armed with two V3C Darter short-range AAMs. The Darter entered SAAF service in 1990 and has an off-boresight capability of 20 degrees when used in conjunction with the Cheetah pilot's helmet-mounted sight.

This Cheetah bears the insignia of No 2 Squadron, South African Air Force, whose home base is Louis Trichardt AFB in the north-east of the country. The single seat Cheetah C was developed in great secrecy, and was eventually revealed in 1995.

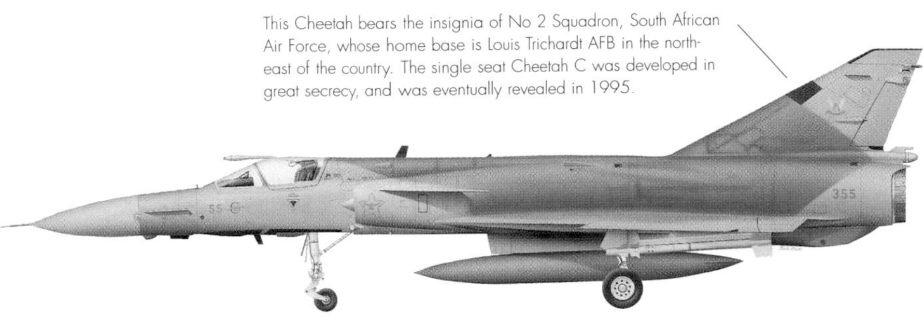

A flight-refuelling probe was one of the first extra items of equipment added by Chile, Israel, Peru, Venezuela and South Africa to their upgraded Mirage aircraft. The South African Air Force uses a number of converted Boeing 707s as tanker aircraft.

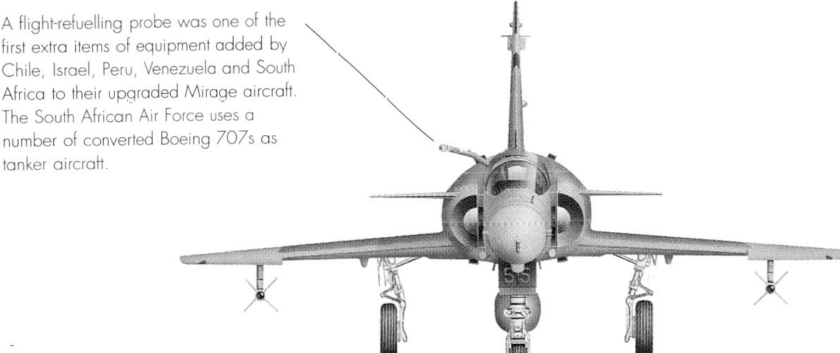

A Swedish Air Force SAAB J-35J displays the aircraft's distinctive shape.

The Draken was designed from the outset to intercept transonic bombers at all altitudes and in all weathers. The first of three prototypes flew for the first time on 25 October 1955, and the initial production version, the J-35A, entered service early in 1960. The major production version of the Draken was the J-35F, which was virtually designed around the Hughes HM-55 Falcon radar-guided air-to-air missile. It was fitted with an improved S7B collision-course fire control system, a high capacity datalink system integrating the aircraft with the STRIL 60 air defence system, an infra red sensor under the nose and PS-01A search and ranging radar. The J-35C was a two-seat operational trainer, while the last new-build variant, the J-35J, was a development of the J-35D with more capable radar, collision-course fire control and a Hughes infrared sensor to operate with the Hughes Falcon AAM. Total production of the Draken was around 600 aircraft, equipping 17 RSAF squadrons. It was also exported to Denmark and Finland. The Draken was the first fully supersonic aircraft in western Europe to be deployed operationally.

Saab J-35J Draken

Type:	single-seat all-weather interceptor
Powerplant:	one 7830kg (17,265lb) Svenska Flygmotor RM6C (licence-built Rolls-Royce Avon 300 series) turbojet
Performance:	maximum speed 2125km/h (1320mph) at altitude; service ceiling 20,000m (65,615ft); range 3250km (2020 miles)
Weights:	empty 7425kg (16,372lb); maximum take-off 16,000kg (35,280lb)
Dimensions:	wing span 9.40m (30ft 10in); length 15.40m (50ft 6.5in); height 3.90m (12ft 9in)
Armament:	one 30mm (1.19in) cannon; four AAMs of various types; up to 4082kg (9000lb) of bombs on attack mission

The Draken was well suited to operations in the far north of Sweden.

SWEDEN

SAAB Viggen about to touch down at the International Air Tattoo in 1999.

One of the most potent combat aircraft of the 1970s, the Saab 37 Viggen (Thunderbolt) was designed to carry out the four roles of attack, interception, reconnaissance and training. Powered by a Swedish version of the Pratt & Whitney JT8D turbofan engine, with a powerful Swedish-developed afterburner, the aircraft had excellent acceleration and climb performance. Part of the requirement was that it should be capable of operating from Swedish motorways. The first of seven prototypes flew for the first time on 8

February 1967, followed by the first production AJ-37 single-seat all-weather attack variant in February 1971. Deliveries of the first of 110 AJ-37s began in June that year. The JA-37 interceptor version of the Viggen (149 built) replaced the J35F Draken; the SF-37 (26 delivered) was a single-seat armed photo-reconnaissance variant; and the SH-37 (26 delivered) was an all-weather maritime version. The SK-37 (18 delivered) was a tandem two-seat trainer, with a secondary attack role. Some Viggens are expected to remain in service until 2010.

Saab SF-37 Viggen

Type:	single-seat all-weather photo-reconnaissance aircraft
Powerplant:	one 12,747kg (28,110lb) thrust Volvo Flygmotor RM8 turbofan
Performance:	maximum speed 2124km/h (1320mph) at altitude; service ceiling 18,290m (60,000ft); combat range 1000km (621 miles)
Weights:	empty 11,800kg (26,015lb); normal take-off 15,000kg (33,069lb)
Dimensions:	wing span 10.60m (34ft 9.25in); length 16.30m (53ft 5.67in); height 5.60m (18ft 4.5in)
Armament:	in secondary attack role, seven external hardpoints with for up to 6000kg (13,230lb) of munitions

This photograph ably demonstrates the Viggen's unique wing planform.

SWEDEN

SAAB JAS-39A GRIPEN

Despite some teething troubles, Saab's JAS-39 Gripen is proving to be an excellent multi-role combat aircraft, and is competing with Eurofighter and Rafale in the lucrative export market.

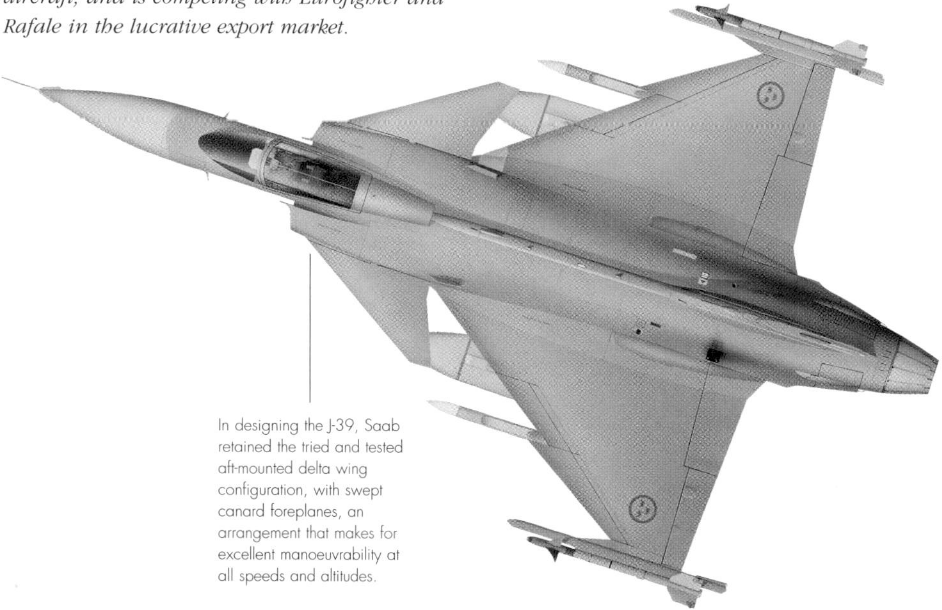

In designing the J-39, Saab retained the tried and tested aft-mounted delta wing configuration, with swept canard foreplanes, an arrangement that makes for excellent manoeuvrability at all speeds and altitudes.

Subdued markings, a very low-visibility colour scheme and the Gripen's small size all combine to make it a difficult opponent in close-in dogfighting. But some pilots have noted that the aircraft's holographic head-up display is so large that it can produce distinctive green flashes of sun 'glint' that are sometimes bright enough to betray the J-39's position.

Carrying a full war load, a Gripen can reach 10,000m (33,000ft) in less than two minutes from starting its take-off roll. At low altitudes the aircraft can reach Mach 1.5, although it needs about 30 seconds to accelerate from Mach 0.5 to Mach 1.5. The aircraft has been flown to Mach 2 at altitude.

This Gripen, which belongs to the Flygvapnet's F7 Wing at Satenas in the country's Southern Air Command, is seen in a mixed attack/defence loadout with two BK90 (DWS 39) glide weapons on the inboard wing pylons and RB99 (AIM-120) AMRAAMs on the outboard pylons. AIM-9 Sidewinders are mounted on the wingtip pylons.

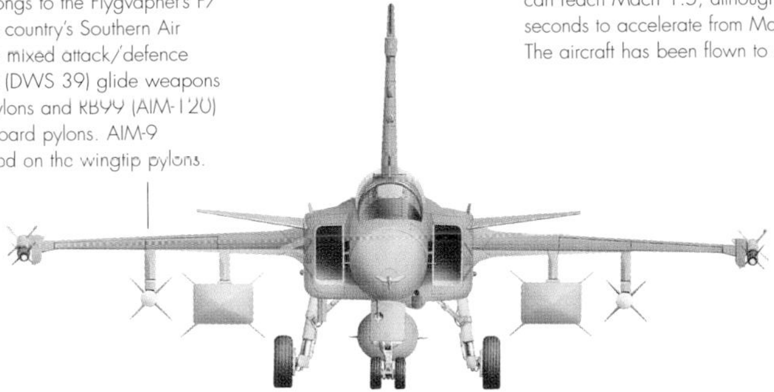

The Ching-Kuo is based on a modified F-16, hence its similar appearance.

The Ching-Kuo was developed with assistance from a number of US companies, including General Dynamics, and resembles a heavily modified F-16. The prototype flew for the first time on 28 May 1989, and was damaged in a landing accident some months later. The second prototype crashed in July 1989, killing its pilot. Despite these mishaps the programme went ahead and the first Ching-Kuo was delivered to the Chinese Nationalist Air Force in 1994, although the lifting of restrictions on the sale of US military aircraft to Taiwan resulted in the original requirement for 250 aircraft being reduced to 130. The Ching-Kuo became operational in 1995, the first two squadrons replacing ageing Northrop F-5 Tigers and Lockheed F-104 Starfighters. The aircraft's development history was plagued by numerous problems, many of which were associated with its 'fly-by-wire' system. The single seat Ching-Kuo was designated F-CK-1A, and a two-seat version F-CK-1B.

AIDC Ching-Kuo F-CK-1B

Type two-seat air defence fighter

Powerplant: two 4291kg (9462lb) thrust ITEC TFE1042-70 turbofans

Performance: maximum speed 1275km/h (792mph) at 10,975m (36,000ft); service ceiling 16,760m (55,000ft); combat radius 1110km (689 miles)

Weights: normal 9072kg (20,000lb) (other data classified)

Dimensions: wing span 9m (29ft 6in); length 14.48m (47ft 6in); height 4.04m (13.3ft)

Armament: one 20mm (0.79in) rotary six-barrel cannon; six pylons for AAMs, AASMs and various combinations of rocket or gun pods

An AIDC Ching-Kuo firing a TC-2 air-to-air missile during a training exercise.

TAIWAN

UNITED KINGDOM

English Electric Canberra B.Mk.6

Originally designed for the radar bombing role, the English Electric Canberra was the greatest success story of Britain's post-war aviation industry and was still in service in the 21st century, more than 50 years after the prototype was rolled out.

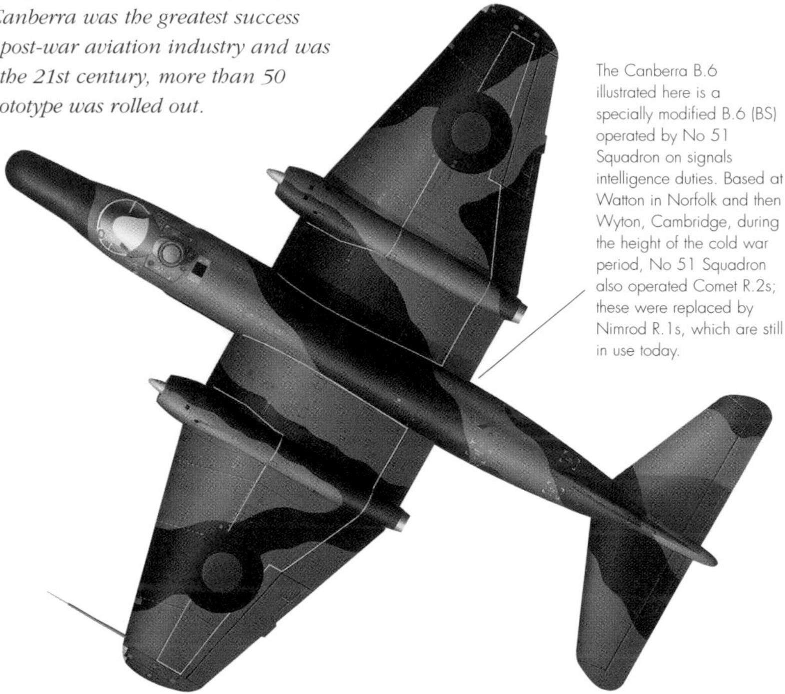

The Canberra B.6 illustrated here is a specially modified B.6 (BS) operated by No 51 Squadron on signals intelligence duties. Based at Watton in Norfolk and then Wyton, Cambridge, during the height of the cold war period, No 51 Squadron also operated Comet R.2s; these were replaced by Nimrod R.1s, which are still in use today.

No 51 Squadron's Canberras appeared very different to standard B.6s, with a modified radome and many extra aerials. Most of these served a variety of Sigint and Elint equipment.

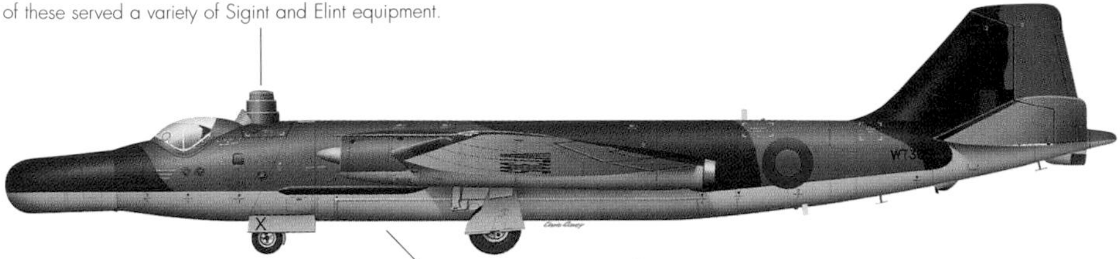

During operational missions, 'Blue Shadow' side-looking airborne radar (SLAR) was used to provide a radar map to fix position before descending to low level to run in towards a target. A typical sortie might involve a high-level approach towards Denmark, then a descent to low level over the Baltic, masked by Oesel Island, to eavesdrop on Soviet signals and radar transmissions.

Extremely accurate navigation was essential when operating close to enemy borders. 'Green Satin' Doppler was used as the primary navigational aid, and was highly prized because of its accuracy and lack of tell-tale emissions.

An Indian Air Force Canberra B(I) Mk.66, refurbished after RAF service.

The first prototype Canberra B.1 flew on 13 May 1949. The first B.2 entered service with No 101 Squadron of RAF Bomber Command in May 1951. A photographic reconnaissance version, the PR.3, was issued to No 540 Squadron in 1953; the PR.7 and PR.9 were two later reconnaissance variants. The next variant was the T.4 dual control trainer, which appeared in 1954; this was followed by the B.6, a more powerful version with Rolls-Royce Avon 109 engines. The B(I)8 featured some radical modifications, the most notable being an entirely redesigned fuselage nose and offset fighter-type cockpit. The B.15, designed for service in the near and far east, was a modified B.6 with underwing hardpoints for bombs or rocket packs. The B.16, for service in Germany, was similar. The Canberra was built under licence in the USA as the Martin B-57, and in Australia as the B.20 and T.21. India was a major export customer, while refurbished Canberras were sold to Argentina (two being lost in the 1982 Falklands war), Chile, Ecuador, France, Peru, Rhodesia/Zimbabwe, South Africa, Sweden, Venezuela and West Germany.

English Electric Canberra B. Mk.6

Type: jet bomber with three crew

Powerplant: two 3397kg (7500lb) thrust Rolls Royce Avon Mk 109 turbojets

Performance: maximum speed 917km/h (570mph) at 12,192m (40,000ft); service ceiling 14,630m (48,000ft); range 4274km (2656 miles)

Weights: empty 11,790kg (26,000lb); maximum take-off 24,925kg (54,950lb)

Dimensions: wing span 19.49m (63ft 11in); length 19.96m (65ft 6in); height 4.78m (15ft 8in)

Armament: up to 2727kg (6000lb) of bombs internally, with provision for 909kg (2000lb) of external munitions

Canberra B.6 WK163 was used as a rocket motor test-bed.

XM967 was the prototype two-seat Lightning T.Mk.5 trainer.

The English Electric Lightning was based on the P.1A research aircraft, but the first operational prototype flew on 4 April 1957, powered by two Rolls-Royce Avons, and exceeded Mach 1.0 on its first flight. On 25 November 1958 it became the first British aircraft to reach Mach 2.0, which it did in level flight. The first production Lightning F.Mk.1 flew on 29 October 1959, and fully combat-equipped Lightnings began entering RAF service in July 1960. The Lightning had a phenomenal initial climb rate of 15,240m (50,000ft) per minute and was constantly improved, evolving via the F.2 and F.3 into the F.6 version. This had a revised wing leading edge designed to reduce subsonic drag and improve range, and was fitted with a large ventral fuel pack which more than doubled capacity. The first Lightning F.6 flew in April 1964 and entered service in the following year. It was the last jet fighter of purely British design, and it was to serve the RAF well in the front line of NATO's air defences until its eventual retirement in 1988.

English Electric Lightning F.2A

Type:	single-seat interceptor
Powerplant:	two 7112kg (15,682lb) thrust Rolls-Royce Avon 211R turbojets
Performance:	maximum speed 2415km/h (1500mph; Mach 2.3) at 12,190m (40,000ft); service ceiling 18,920m (62,000ft) plus; range 1287km (800 miles)
Weights:	empty 12,700kg (28,000lb); maximum take-off 22,680kg (50,000lb)
Dimensions:	wing span 10.61m (34ft 10in); length 16.84m (5ft 3in); height 5.97m (19ft 7in)
Armament:	two nose-mounted 30mm (1.19in) guns; two AAMs

This striking photograph shows Lightnings of No 23 Squadron over a magnificent cloudscape.

UNITED KINGDOM

GLOSTER JAVELIN FAW MK 9

The Gloster Javelin Mk 9 was the ultimate development of Gloster's radical delta, which was a major departure from conventional fighter design when it first appeared.

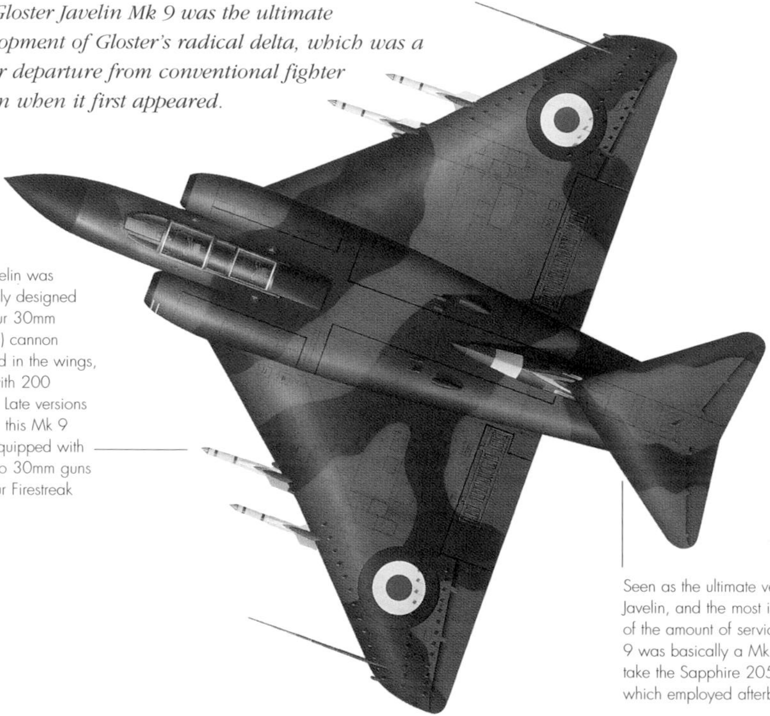

The Javelin was originally designed with four 30mm (1.19in) cannon mounted in the wings, each with 200 rounds. Late versions such as this Mk 9 were equipped with only two 30mm guns and four Firestreak AAMs.

Seen as the ultimate version of the Javelin, and the most important in terms of the amount of service it saw, the Mk 9 was basically a Mk 7 converted to take the Sapphire 205/206 (As.7) which employed afterburning.

The markings displayed on No 11 Squadron's Javelin FAW.9s were quite different from those on its earlier FAW.4s and 5s. They consisted of a strip across the fin and rudder, divided into black and yellow so that the yellow formed a pennant. The two eagles, a feature of the squadron crest, were added in 1964. The motto of No 11 Squadron, which in 2002 was a Tornado F.3 unit, is Ociores acrierosque aquilis (Swifter and keener than eagles).

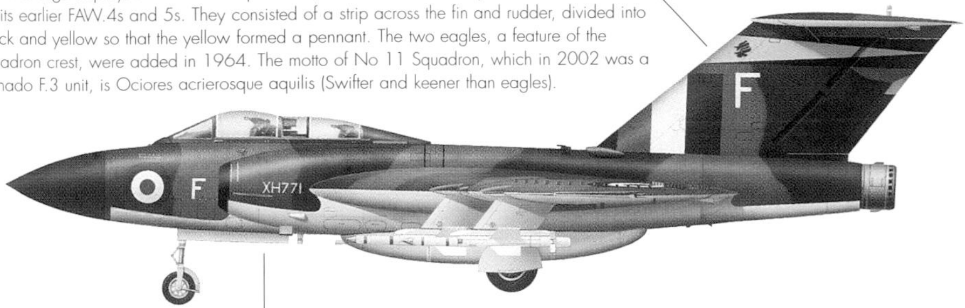

The Javelin pictured here is in the markings of No 11 Squadron, which took over the crews and FAW.9s of No 25 Squadron, relocated from Leuchars in Scotland to Geilenkirchen in Germany on 13 December 1962. No 11 operated a battle flight consisting of two aircraft that were on immediate alert 24 hours a day, 365 days a year, ready to intercept potentially hostile aircraft entering western air space from eastern Europe.

UNITED KINGDOM

Gloster Meteor NF.14

The Gloster Meteor NF.14 was the last of the piloted Meteors (there were some target drone variants subsequently) and was aesthetically the most pleasing. It filled the gap until the deployment of the Gloster Javelin.

Like all the armed Meteor variants, the NF.Mk.14 was equipped with four Hispano 20mm (0.79in) cannon, which were wing-mounted in the night fighters because of the nose radar. The Mk V cannon on the NF.14 were each provided with 160 rounds.

Based on the Meteor T.7 airframe, the Meteor night fighter family, beginning with the NF.11, shared the trainer's wing, but featured a new tail unit derived from the F.Mk.8 and a lengthened nose to accommodate the AI radar equipment. Cabin pressurization was a new feature, as was the clear-view bubble canopy. The NF.14 was not fitted with ejection seats.

The NF.14 seen here, WS800, like all other Meteor night fighters, was built by W.G. Armstrong Whitworth. It is shown in the markings of the commanding officer of No 60 Squadron, the last RAF Meteor squadron to form, in 1959. Assigned to the Far East Air Force and stationed at Seletar, Singapore, No 60 was the last front-line squadron to operate the Meteor, converting to Gloster Javelins in 1961.

Meteor NF.14s routinely carried three external fuel tanks, two under the wings and one belly tank, with a total capacity of 1705 litres (375 Imp gal).

UNITED KINGDOM

HAWKER HUNTER T.MK.8

One of the most graceful combat aircraft ever built, the Hawker Hunter was a huge success. In a career spanning a quarter of a century it equipped 30 RAF fighter squadrons, in addition to numerous units of foreign air forces.

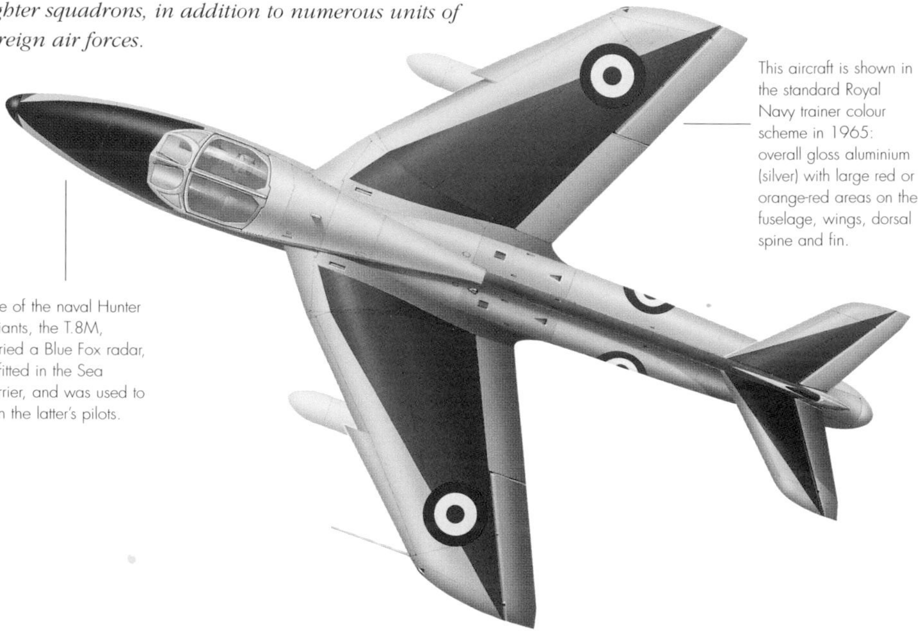

This aircraft is shown in the standard Royal Navy trainer colour scheme in 1965: overall gloss aluminium (silver) with large red or orange-red areas on the fuselage, wings, dorsal spine and fin.

One of the naval Hunter variants, the T.8M, carried a Blue Fox radar, as fitted in the Sea Harrier, and was used to train the latter's pilots.

The Hunter T.Mk.8 seen here, XL598 of No 738 Naval Air Squadron, was based at RNAS Brawdy in 1965. It began life as one of a batch of ten new-build Mk.8s (actually ordered as T.7s for the RAF) and made its first flight on 15 October 1958. The aircraft is marked with Brawdy's 'BY' code and the Pegasus from its squadron emblem.

Like the RAF's T.Mk.7, the Mk.8 featured a four-pylon Mod 228 wing with a 'dog tooth' leading edge. A single 30mm (1.19in) Aden gun was also fitted, although the aircraft differed from the Mk.7 in having an arrester hook.

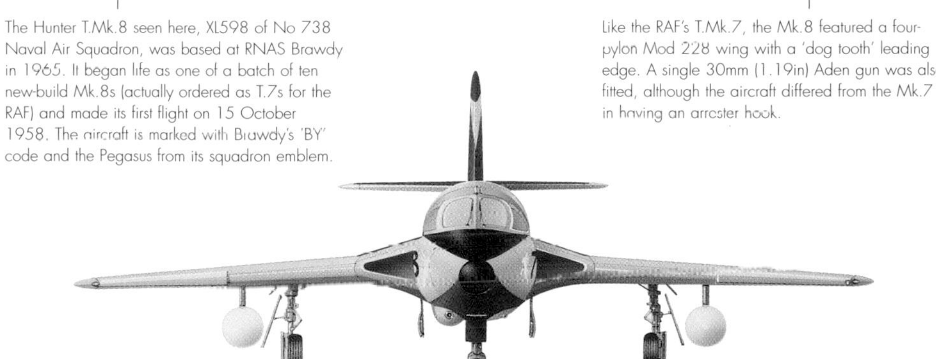

T.Mk.7s pictured over the North Sea while operating from RAF Lossiemouth.

Designed to replace the Meteor, the prototype Hunter (P.1067) flew on 20 July 1951. The F.Mk.1, which entered service in 1954, suffered from engine problems in high-altitude gun firing trials, resulting in some modifications to its Rolls-Royce Avon turbojet. These modifications (along with increased fuel capacity and provision for underwing tanks) produced the Hunter F.4, which went on to equip the 2nd Tactical Air Force in Germany. The Hunter Mks 2 and 5 were powered by the Armstrong Siddeley Sapphire engine.

Deliveries of the Hunter F.Mk.6 (equipped with the large 4535kg [10,000lb] thrust Avon 203 engine) began in 1956 and the F.6 went on to equip 15 squadrons of RAF Fighter Command. The Hunter FGA.9 was a development of the F.6 optimized for ground attack. Hunter Mks 7, 8, 12, T52, T62, T66, T67 and T69 were all two-seat trainer variants. The FR.10 was a fighter-reconnaissance version, and the GA.11 was an operational trainer for the Royal Navy. The aircraft was licence-built in Holland and Belgium; principal customers for British-built aircraft were India, Switzerland and Sweden. The grand total of Hunter production, including two-seat trainers, was 1972 aircraft.

Hawker Hunter T.Mk.8

Type:	two-seat advanced trainer
Powerplant:	one 3628kg (8000lb) thrust Rolls-Royce Avon 122 turbojet
Performance:	maximum speed 1117km/h (694mph); service ceiling 14,325m (47,000ft); range 689km (429 miles)
Weights:	empty 6406kg (14,122lb); maximum take-off 7802kg (17,200lb)
Dimensions:	wing span 10.26m (33ft 8in); length 14.89m (48ft 10in); height 4.02m (13ft 2in)
Armament:	one 30mm (1.19in) cannon; pylons for two 453kg (1000lb) bombs and 24 76cm (3in) rockets

A Hunter T.Mk.75A in the markings of No 14 Squadron of the Republic of Singapore Air Force.

UNITED KINGDOM

UNITED STATES

BELL V-22 OSPREY

From an interesting experiment the Bell V-22 Osprey tilt-rotor aircraft has evolved into a valuable operational asset, able to fly faster and for longer than most helicopters, while still retaining the ability to take off and land vertically.

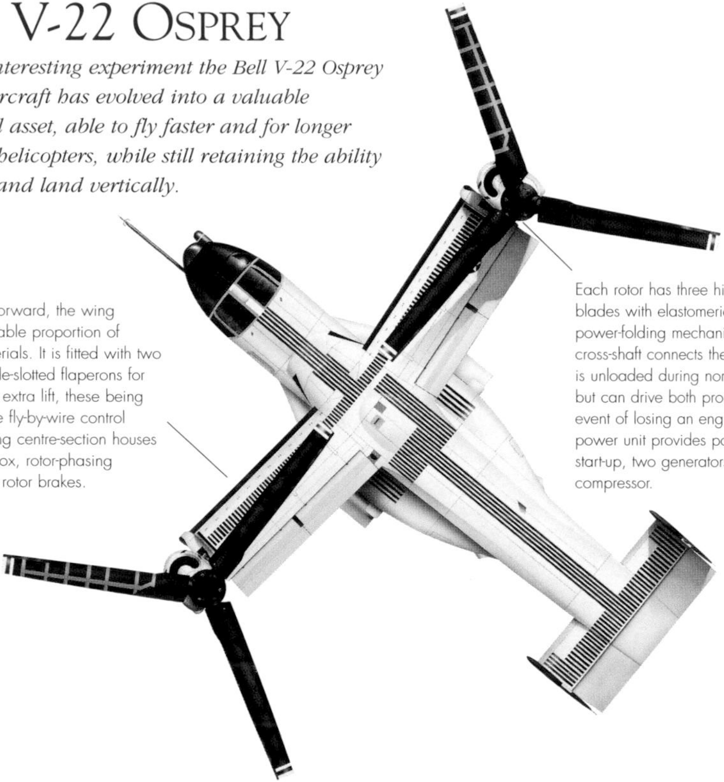

Slightly swept forward, the wing contains a sizeable proportion of composite materials. It is fitted with two sections of single-slotted flaperons for roll control and extra lift, these being operated by the fly-by-wire control system. The wing centre-section houses the drive gearbox, rotor-phasing equipment and rotor brakes.

Each rotor has three high-twist tapered blades with elastomeric bearings and a power-folding mechanism. A transverse cross-shaft connects the two rotors and is unloaded during normal operations, but can drive both proprotors in the event of losing an engine. An auxiliary power unit provides power for engine start-up, two generators and an air compressor.

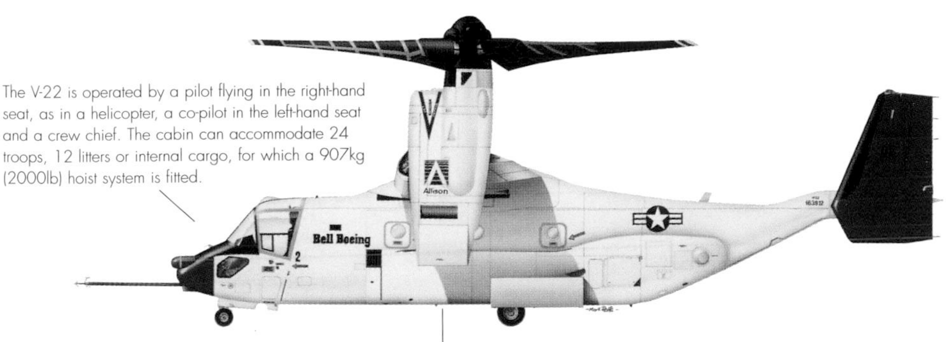

The V-22 is operated by a pilot flying in the right-hand seat, as in a helicopter, a co-pilot in the left-hand seat and a crew chief. The cabin can accommodate 24 troops, 12 litters or internal cargo, for which a 907kg (2000lb) hoist system is fitted.

Allison won the competition to power the V-22 with its T406-AD-400 engine, based on the well-tried and proven T56 turboprop. Each engine is fitted with a Lucas FADEC system with analogue backup and is mounted in a Bell-built tilting nacelle.

The Bell V-22 owes its existence to the Bell XV-15 tilt-rotor testbed aircraft, developed in the mid-1970s. The XV-15 was powered by two Lycoming T-53 turboshaft engines driving three-bladed 7.62m (25ft) metal rotors; the engines were located in wingtip nacelles. For take-off, the engine/rotor assembly operated vertically,

The Bell V-22 Osprey has brought a new dimension to assault operations.

generating downward thrust and enabling the aircraft to lift off like a helicopter. Once off the ground, it could either fly like a helicopter or as a conventional aircraft, the engine/rotor assembly tilting horizontally in the latter case. The XV-15's successful test programme led to the development of the V-22 Osprey V/STOL assault aircraft, which flew for the first time on 19 March 1989.

OPERATIONAL SERVICE

The aircraft entered service in 1997 and is available in three configurations for the US Services: the CV-22 for long-range missions on behalf of the USAF's Special Operations Command, the MV-22 combat assault vehicle for the US Marine Corps, and the HV-22 for combat search and rescue, special

Bell/Boeing V-22 Osprey (CV-22)

Type:	V/STOL transport with three crew
Powerplant:	two 4586 kW (6150hp) Allison T406-AD-400 turboshaft engines
Performance:	maximum speed 556km/h (345mph); service ceiling 7930m (26,000ft); range 3892km (2418 miles)
Weights:	empty 15,032kg (33,142lb); maximum take-off 27,406kg (60,500lb)
Dimensions:	wing span 14.36m (47ft 1in); length 19.09m (62ft 8in); rotor diameter 11.58m (38ft)
Armament:	none

warfare, and fleet logistic support. The aircraft can carry 24 troops.

This Osprey is shown during the transition from vertical to forward flight.

UNITED STATES

Boeing E-3 Sentry

The Boeing E-3A Sentry, developed during the Cold War, has since proved an enormous asset in the Gulf, the former Yugoslavia and Afghanistan.

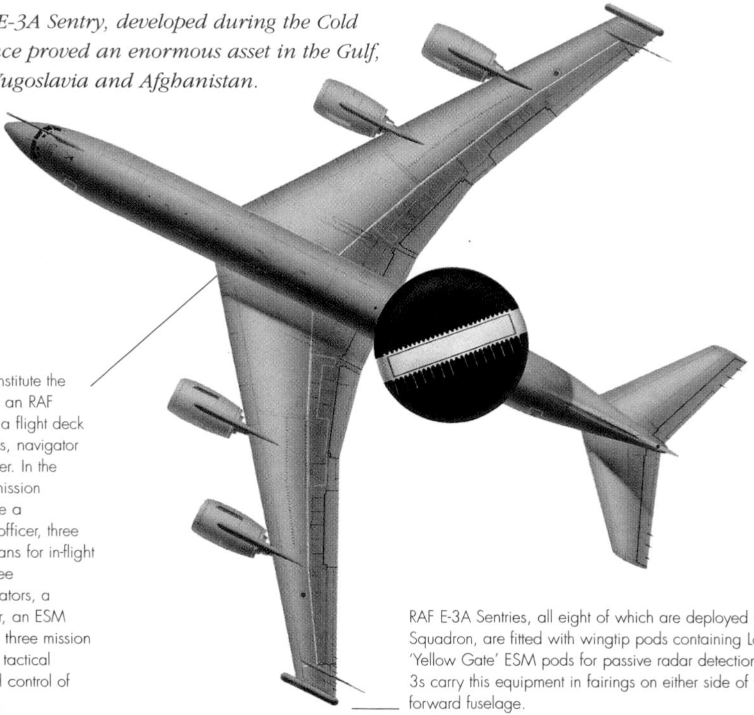

17 personnel constitute the standard crew of an RAF Sentry, including a flight deck crew of two pilots, navigator and flight engineer. In the main cabin 13 mission operatives include a communications officer, three airborne technicians for in-flight maintenance, three surveillance operators, a datalink manager, an ESM systems operator, three mission specialists and a tactical director in overall control of the mission crew.

RAF E-3A Sentries, all eight of which are deployed with No 8 Squadron, are fitted with wingtip pods containing Loral 1017 'Yellow Gate' ESM pods for passive radar detection. USAF E-3s carry this equipment in fairings on either side of the forward fuselage.

UK and French E-3s are fitted with flight refuelling probes, offset to starboard, although the receptacle for the US boom system is retained in the upper forward fuselage.

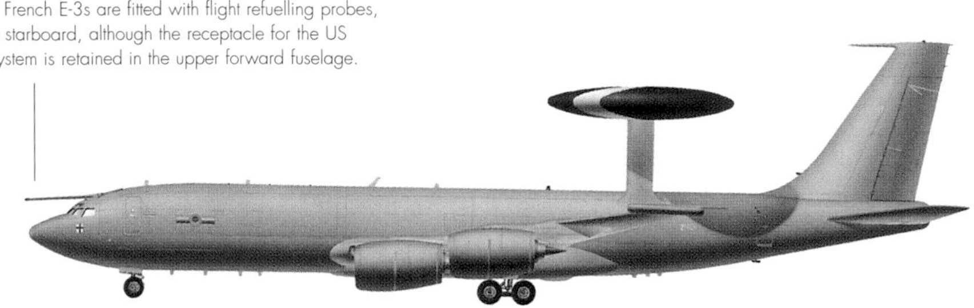

The rotodome measures 1.83m (6ft) in depth and 9.14m (30ft) in diameter. It rotates at six rpm when in use and ¼rpm when dormant in order to keep the bearings lubricated. Contained within is the Westinghouse APY-2 radar and IFF/TADIL-C array. The radar 'eye' scans through 360 degrees and can 'see' more than 320 kilometres (200 miles).

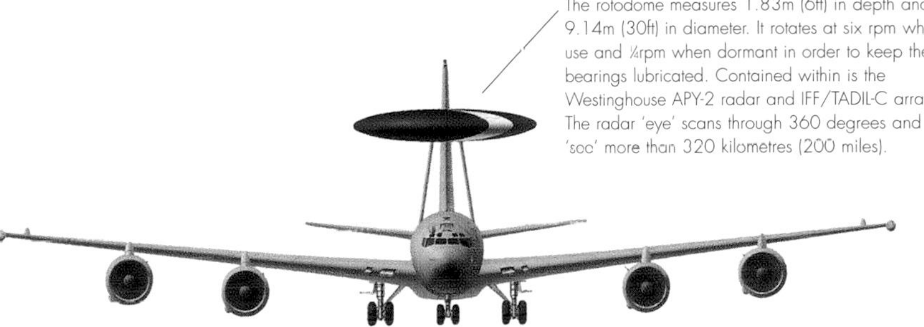

UNITED STATES

Boeing/Grumman E-8 J-Stars

During the Gulf War, the USAF introduced a new aircraft to track down Iraqi missiles in the famous 'Scud Hunt'. This was the E-8A Joint Surveillance Target Attack Radar System, or J-Stars.

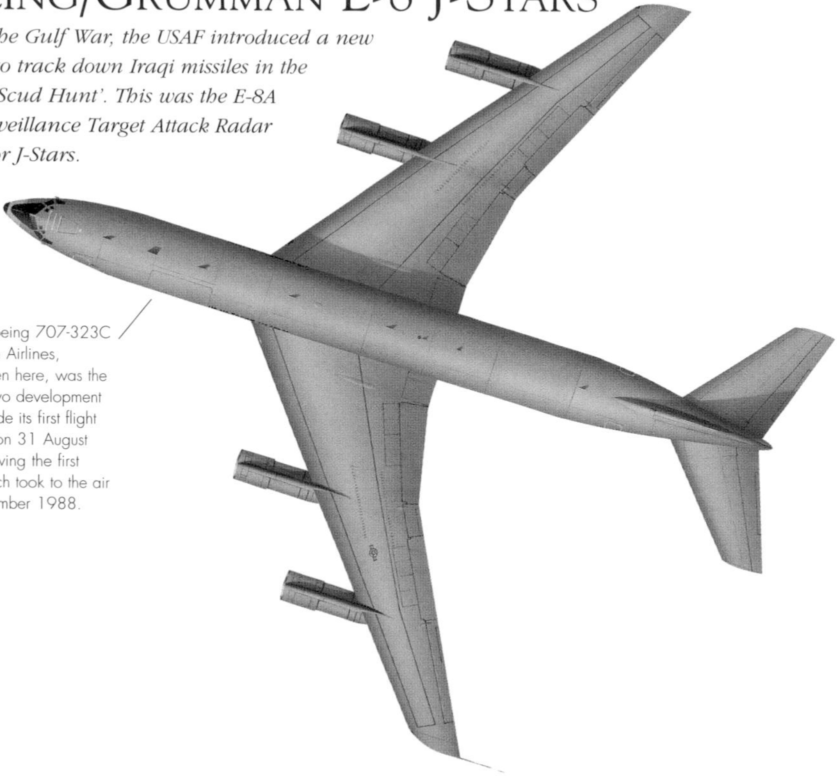

Built as a Boeing 707-323C for American Airlines, N8411, seen here, was the second of two development E-8As. It made its first flight as an E-8A on 31 August 1989, following the first aircraft, which took to the air on 22 December 1988.

As the E-8As carried so much test equipment, the number of operator consoles within the cabin was reduced to ten. The E-8C has 17 consoles, plus one for the management of defensive electronics.

On a standard mission the E-8 carries a crew of 21, comprising three flight crew and 19 systems operators. On a long endurance mission this is increased to 34, with six flight crew and 28 systems operators.

The large 'teardrop' fairing under the E-8A's centre section housed the antenna for the Flight Test Data Link. Fitted to test aircraft only, it was used during Operation Desert Storm for transmitting data over long distances back to central commands in Saudi Arabia.

At the design stage of the CH-113 the main objective was to take full advantage of the high power, small size and light weight of the shaft-turbine engines then becoming available. The traditional Vertol tandem-rotor layout was retained, and the turbines were mounted above the rear of the cabin on each side of the aft rotor pylon. This arrangement gave the maximum unobstructed cabin area and permitted the use of a large rear ramp for the straight-in loading of vehicles and bulky freight. The standard commercial version

A CH-113 sporting the bright yellow colour of search and rescue helicopters.

was the Model 107, and following extensive experience in North America, Europe and the Far East, several advanced versions were produced.These included the CH/UH-46 Sea Knight for the US Navy. The CH-113 was based on this, but with various modifications that included extra fuel tankage. Six CH-113 Labrador utility models were delivered to the Royal Canadian Air Force in 1963-64 for search and rescue duties, while the Canadian Army received 12 CH-113A Voyageurs as troop and cargo carriers in 1964-65.The CH-113s performed well in Canadian service, the twin-engine design ensuring reliability under difficult conditions in the frozen north.

Boeing CH-113 Labrador

Type:	utility helicopter with three crew
Powerplant:	two 932kW (1250hp) General Electric T58-GE-8B shaft turbines
Performance:	maximum speed 270km/h (168mph); service ceiling 3430m (11,250ft); range 751km (467 miles)
Weights:	empty 5104kg (11,251lb); maximum take-off 9706kg (21,400lb)
Dimensions:	main rotor diameter 15.24m (50ft); length of fuselage 13.59m (44ft 7in); height to top of rear rotor hub 5.09m (16ft 8.5in)
Armament:	none

Although based on the US Navy's CH-46 Sea Knight helicopter, the CH-113 had various subtle modifications.

The Cessna O-2 was a military version of the Cessna Model 337 Super Skymaster, which had gone into production for the civilian market in 1965. Its twin tail booms and tractor-pusher (pull-push) propeller arrangement were distinctive. In 1966 the USAF selected the O-2 military variant to supplement the O-1 Bird Dog forward air controller (FAC) aircraft then operating in Southeast Asia. Its twin engines enabled the O-2 to absorb ground fire and still get home safely, making it well liked by its crews. The O-2 first flew in

The Cessna O-2 was extremely well equipped with communications gear.

January 1967 and production deliveries began in March. Production ended in June 1970 after 532 O-2s had been built for the USAF. Two models were produced; the O-2A, which was equipped with wing pylons to carry rockets, flares and other ordnance, and which was used for marking enemy targets and co-ordinating air strikes, and the O-2B, which was a psychological warfare aircraft equipped with loudspeakers and leaflet dispensers. This model carried no ordnance. O-2As were often used in conjunction with C-130 gunships in night operations along the Ho Chi Minh Trail, and others were used on clandestine missions over Laos.

Cessna O-2A Super Skymaster

Type: two-seat forward air control aircraft

Powerplant: two 157kW (210hp) Continental 10-360 air-cooled engines

Performance: maximum speed 320km/h (199mph) at sea level; service ceiling 5880m (19,300ft); range 2164km (1345 miles)

Weights: empty 1206kg (2660lb); maximum take-off 2013kg (4440lb)

Dimensions: wing span 11.63m (38ft 2in); length 9.07m (29ft 9in); height 2.84m (9ft 4in)

Armament: pylons for various munitions, including rockets, flares and 7.62mm (0.30in) Minigun pack

This O-2A is armed with pods containing 28 folding-fin aircraft rockets (FFARs).

The first supersonic bomber to enter service anywhere in the world, the Convair B-58 originated in an Air Force design competition of 1949, which was won by the Fort Worth Division of General Dynamics. The aircraft was ordered into production in October 1954, and the prototype flew on 11 November 1956. The aircraft was intended to replace the B-47, but in the end only two Bomb Wings, the 43rd and 305th, were equipped with it, the first operational Hustler entering service with Strategic Air Command's 43rd Bomb

The B-58 Hustler's high accident rate ensured that it saw only limited service.

Wing in March 1960. The three-man crew occupied tandem cockpits, and the B-58 was the first aircraft in the world in which the crew had individual escape capsules for use at supersonic speeds. Weapons and extra fuel were carried in a large, jettisonable under-fuselage pod. The only production version was the B-58A; 103 were built, eight being converted as TB-58 trainers. In an operational career lasting ten years, from 1960 to 1970, the B-58 established several records.

Convair B-58A Hustler

Type:	strategic bomber with three crew
Powerplant:	four 7075kg (15,600lb) thrust General Electric J79-GE-5 turbojets
Performance:	maximum speed 2228km/h (1385mph) at 12,190m (40,000ft); service ceiling 19,500m (64,000ft); range 8248km (5125 miles)
Weights:	empty 25,200kg (55,560lb); maximum take-off 72,576kg (160,000lb)
Dimensions:	wing span 17.32m (56ft 10in); length 29.49m (96ft 9in); height 9.58m (31ft 5in)
Armament:	one 20mm (0.79in) Vulcan six-barrel cannon; 8820kg (19,450lb) of nuclear or conventional bombs

The B-58's under-fuselage pod contained both fuel and weapons.

A Convair F-106 test-launching a Genie nuclear-tipped AAM.

The design of the Convair F-102 was based on experience gained in flight testing of the XF-92 delta-wing research aircraft. Two prototype YF-102s were built, the first flying on 24 October 1953. This aircraft was damaged beyond repair only a week later, but testing resumed with the second machine in January 1954. Eight more YF-102s were built for evaluation, and it soon became apparent that the aircraft's performance fell short of expectations. After substantial airframe redesign the machine re-emerged in

December 1954 as the YF-102A, and the type was ordered into full production. Meanwhile, work was proceeding on a more advanced version, the Convair F-102B, whose prototype flew on 26 December 1956. This was followed by 16 pre-production aircraft, which were used for trials and evaluation. The first production F-106 entered service with the 539th Fighter Interceptor Squadron in June 1959 and production ended in 1962 after 257 aircraft had been built, equipping 13 fighter interceptor squadrons. In the early 1960s the F-106A was the most important aircraft on the inventory of Air Defense Command, and several units of the Air National Guard also flew it.

Convair F-106A Delta Dart

Type:	all-weather interceptor
Powerplant:	one 11,113kg (24,500lb) thrust Pratt & Whitney J75-P-17 turbojet
Performance:	maximum speed 1328km/h (825mph) at 10,970m (36,000ft); service ceiling 16,460m (54,000ft); range 2172km (1350 miles)
Weights:	empty 10,712kg (23,616lb); maximum take-off 18,949kg (41,775lb)
Dimensions:	wing span 11.66m (38ft 3in); length: 21.58m (70ft 9in); height 6.18m (20ft 3in)
Armament:	one unguided AAM with a 1.5kT yield nuclear warhead, four infrared homing AAMs; unguided AAM later replaced by 20mm (0.79in) cannon

A Convair F-106A of the 49th Fighter Interceptor Squadron taxies in.

UNITED STATES

Douglas A-4E Skyhawk

One of the most versatile combat aircraft ever produced, the Douglas A-4 Skyhawk was designed to replace the piston-engined A4D Skyraider, which had performed vital tasks in the Korean War.

The A-4E was the first variant to be powered by the Pratt & Whitney J52, providing an extra 317kg (700lb) of thrust compared to the earlier Wright J65.

Wearing the markings of VA-72 'Blue Hawks', this A-4E Skyhawk served aboard the carrier USS *Independence* in the South China Sea during May 1965. As a result of their long and active combat life, more A-4s were lost during the Vietnam War than any other type of carrier-based aircraft, accounting for nearly 37 per cent of USN combat losses. In all, 196 USN A-4s were lost in combat, and 77 in operational accidents.

The A-4E carried a pair of 20mm (0.79in) Colt Mk 12 cannon mounted in the wing roots, and staggered in order to provide clearance for the magazines within the fuselage.

This A-4E is armed with six 227kg (500lb) Mk 82 Snakeye retarded bombs. These enabled the aircraft to deliver the weapons from low level and still escape the blast.

First flown on 23 April 1956, the giant C-133 was originally conceived as a means of transporting the American intercontinental ballistic missiles (ICBMs) and intermediate range ballistic missiles that were under development. There were no prototypes, and the Cargomaster went straight into production as the C-133A. It entered service with the USAF Military Air Transport Service in 1957 and equipped the 1st, 39th and 84th Air Transport Squadrons, 35 being built. The C-133A was followed by 15 C-133Bs, with more powerful engines.

The C-133 was originally designed to carry intercontinental ballistic missiles.

The C-133 featured a high-mounted wing, blister fairings on either side of the fuselage to accommodate the landing gear, and both rear-loading and side-loading cargo doors. The cargo compartment was pressurized, heated and ventilated. The C-133 could accommodate 49,880kg (110,000lb) of cargo or a fully assembled Thor, Jupiter or Atlas missile. As an alternative, the cargo hold could be fitted with 200 airline-type seats for troop transportation. By 1958 the C-133s were operating on Military Air Transport Service routes throughout the world. The fleet was withdrawn from service in 1971 because of fatigue problems, after rendering invaluable service in the Vietnam War.

Douglas C-133A Cargomaster

Type:	heavy lift transport with 10 crew
Powerplant:	four 4847kW (6500hp) Pratt & Whitney T34-P-7WA turboprops
Performance:	maximum speed 571km/h (355mph); service ceiling 5915m (19,400ft); range 6395km (3975 miles) with a 23,556kg (52,000lb) load
Weights:	empty 50,662kg (111,700lb); maximum take-off 143,600kg (316,600lb)
Dimensions:	wing span 54.76m (179ft 8in); length 48.0m (157ft 6in); height 11.98m (39ft 3in)
Armament:	none

With its massive troop- and cargo-carrying capacity, the C-133 was invaluable during the Vietnam war.

UNITED STATES

UNITED STATES

Fairchild Republic A-10 Thunderbolt II

In December 1970 Fairchild Republic and Northrop were each selected to build a prototype of a new close support aircraft for evaluation under the USAF's A-X programme. The winner was Fairchild Republic's formidable Thunderbolt II.

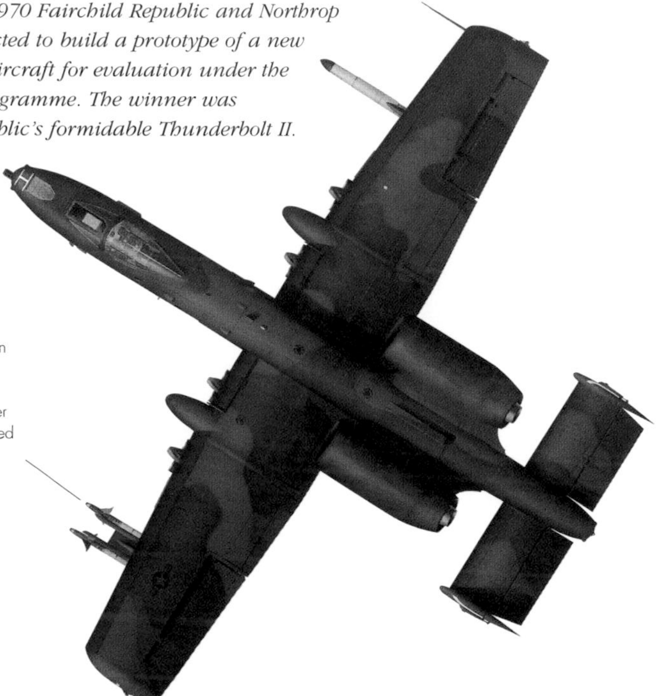

This aircraft carries an ALQ-184 ECM pod and two AIM-9L Sidewinders, the latter on an ANG-developed Dual Rail Adaptor (DRA).

This OA-10A carries the 'PA' tailcode of the 103rd Fighter Squadron, 111th Fighter Group of the Pennsylvania Air National Guard. This unit was rare in being an FAC specialist, and was equipped solely with OA-10As. It completed conversion in December 1989, having earlier flown Cessna OA-37Bs, and Cessna O-2As before that.

The aircraft depicted here is an OA-10A, which was identical to the A-10A except for its assigned mission, which was Forward Air Control (FAC). In practice, all Thunderbolt IIs were capable of carrying out FAC tasks.

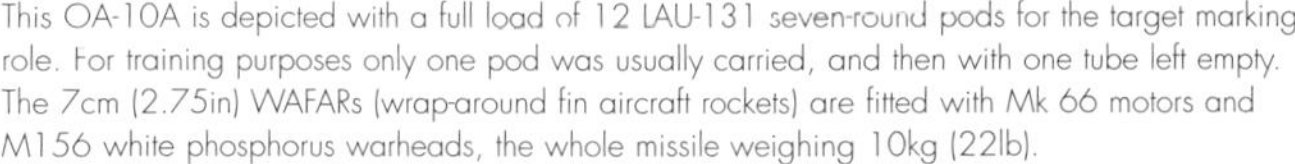

This OA-10A is depicted with a full load of 12 LAU-131 seven-round pods for the target marking role. For training purposes only one pod was usually carried, and then with one tube left empty. The 7cm (2.75in) WAFARs (wrap-around fin aircraft rockets) are fitted with Mk 66 motors and M156 white phosphorus warheads, the whole missile weighing 10kg (22lb).

The core of the A-10's built-in firepower is its massive GAU-8/A seven-barrel 30mm (1.19in) rotary cannon, mounted on the centreline under the forward fuselage. The A-10 was designed to operate from short, unprepared strips less than 457m (1,500ft) long. The first A-10s were delivered in March 1977 and altogether

Heavily armed, the A-10's key weapon is its seven-barrel rotary cannon.

the USAF took delivery of 727 aircraft. The A-10 has a combat radius of 403km (250 miles), enough to reach a target area on the East German border from central Germany and then move on to another target area in northern Germany. The aircraft has a three and a half hour loiter endurance, although operational war sorties in Europe would probably have lasted between one and two hours. In general, operations by A-10s envisaged co-operation with US Army helicopters; the latter would hit the mobile SAM and AAA systems accompanying a Soviet armoured thrust, leaving the A-10s free to concentrate their fire on the tanks. Twelve years later, these tactics were used to deadly effect in the 1991 Gulf War, and in NATO operations over the former Yugoslavia.

Fairchild Republic A-10A Thunderbolt II

Type:	single-seat close support and assault aircraft
Powerplant:	two 4112kg (9067lb) thrust General Electric TF34-GE-100 turbofans
Performance:	maximum speed 706km/h (439mph); service ceiling 7625m (25,000ft); combat radius 403km (250 miles)
Weights:	empty 11,321kg (24,963lb); maximum take-off 22,680kg (50,000lb)
Dimensions:	wing span 17.53m (57ft 6in); length 16.26m (53ft 4in); height 4.47m (14ft 8in)
Armament:	one 30mm (1.19in) cannon; 11 hardpoints for up to 7528kg (16,000lb) of ordnance

The high-mounted cockpit gives the A-10 pilot an unrivalled all-round view.

UNITED STATES

An EF-111A Raven of the 42nd Electronic Warfare Squadron over Oxfordshire.

Development of the EF-111A Raven electronic support aircraft began in January 1975, when the USAF contracted with Grumman Aerospace to modify two F-111As to serve as electronic warfare platforms. The aircraft's high speed, long range and substantial payload made it ideally suited to this role. To accommodate the extra 2718kg (6000lb) of equipment Grumman added a 4.88m (16ft) canoe-type radome under the fuselage and a pod mounted on top of the tail fin. Both EF-111A conversions flew in 1977, and after two years of flight tests authority was given for the conversion of 42 aircraft. The first production EF-111A was delivered to the 388th Tactical Electronic Squadron in November 1981, and the type was declared fully operational in 1983.The EF-111A Raven first entered the public eye in April 1986, when UK-based aircraft provided jamming support for F-111E fighter-bombers attacking targets in Libya in response to that nation's alleged support for terrorist activities. The last EF-111As were withdrawn in 1999.

General Dynamics/Grumman EF-111A Raven

Type: two-seat electronic warfare aircraft

Powerplant: two 8380kg (18,500lb) thrust Pratt & Whitney TF-30-P3 turbofans

Performance: maximum speed 2272km/h (1412mph); service ceiling 13,725m (45,000ft); combat radius 1495km (929 miles)

Weights: empty 25,067kg (55,275lb); maximum take-off 40,337kg (88,928lb)

Dimensions: wing span 19.2m (63ft) spread; length 23.18m (76ft); height 6.1m (20ft)

Armament: two AIM-9L Sidewinders on pylons (optional)

Its numerous electronic bulges gave the EF-111A an ungainly appearance.

UNITED STATES

A US Navy Grumman A-6 Intruder launching a SLAM attack missile.

Designed as a carrier-based low-level attack bomber with the ability to deliver both nuclear and conventional warloads with pinpoint accuracy in all weathers, the Grumman A-6 was the winner among 11 competitors in a US Navy design contest of 1957. The A-6A prototype flew on 19 April 1960 and the first operational aircraft entered service on 1 February 1963. The last delivery took place in December 1969, by which time 488 had been built. The A-6A saw extensive action over Vietnam and also participated in later actions, such as the strike on Libya in April 1986. The next variant was the EA-6A electronic warfare aircraft, 27 of which were produced for the US Marine Corps; this was followed by the EA-6B Prowler, with advanced avionics and a longer nose section to accommodate two extra ECM specialists. The last attack variant was the A-6E, which first flew in February 1970; total procurement orders called for 318 A-6Es, including 119 converted from A-6As. Other conversions of the basic A-6A were the A-6C, with enhanced night attack capability, and the KA-6D flight refuelling tanker.

Grumman A-6A Intruder

Type:	two-seat all-weather strike aircraft
Powerplant:	two 4218kg (9300lb) Pratt & Whitney J52-P-8A turbojets
Performance:	maximum speed 1043km/h (648mph); service ceiling 14,480m (47,500ft); combat range 1627km (1011 miles)
Weights:	empty 12,132kg (26,746lb); maximum take-off 27,397kg (60,400lb)
Dimensions:	wing span 16.15m (53ft); length 16.64m (54ft 7in); height 4.93m (16ft 2in)
Armament:	five external hardpoints for up to 8165kg (18,000lb) of ordnance

The A-6E, seen here, first flew in February 1970 and was to be the last attack variant of the Intruder.

Grumman EA-6B Prowler

During Operation Desert Storm in 1991, one of the Allies' greatest assets was the Grumman EA-6 Prowler electronic warfare aircraft, which played a key part in suppressing Iraqi radar systems.

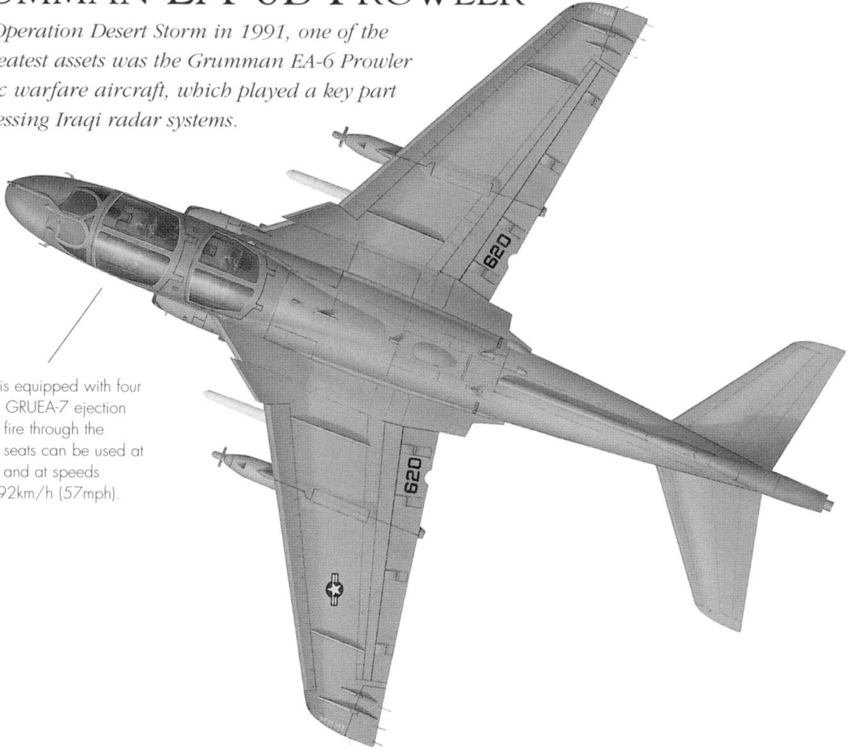

The Prowler is equipped with four Martin-Baker GRUEA-7 ejection seats, which fire through the canopy. The seats can be used at ground level and at speeds upwards of 92km/h (57mph).

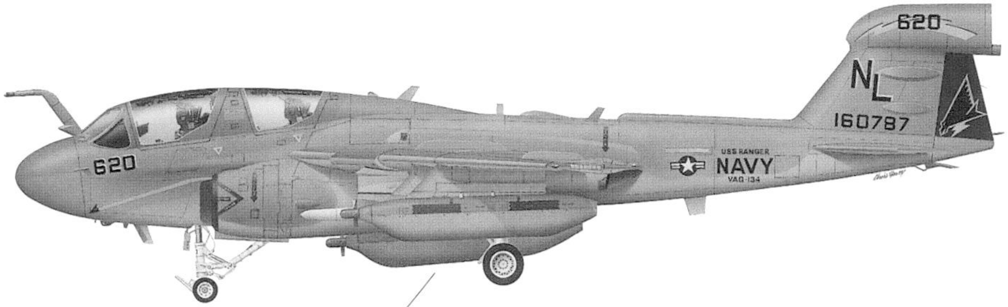

The Prowler is designed to carry up to five AN/ALQ-99 jamming pods on its four underwing and single centreline stations. It can also carry a maximum of four AGM-88 HARM missiles. Beyond this, the only other external stores cleared for EA-6B carriage are standard twin-finned Aero 1D fuel tanks, AN/ALE-41 chaff pods and CNU-188A baggage pods.

The bulged fibreglass fin-tip fairing for the Prowler's AN/ALQ-99F system has long been known as the 'football'. The Tactical Jamming System receivers in the 'football' cover frequency bands are distinct from those covered by the other onboard antennae, such as the twin blister antennae below the 'football' on either side of the fin.

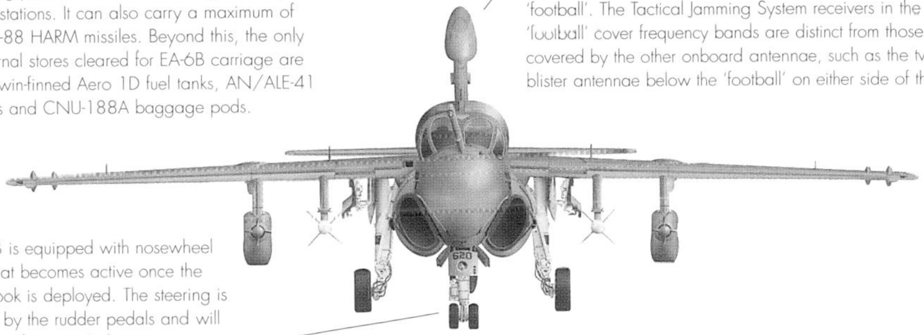

The EA-6B is equipped with nosewheel steering that becomes active once the arrester hook is deployed. The steering is controlled by the rudder pedals and will allow turns of up to 60 degrees.

The first twenty E-2As were used for service evaluation and carrier trials, and the type was formally accepted into US Navy service in January 1964, when it began to equip Early Warning Squadron VAW-11 at San Diego. This unit went to sea with its Hawkeyes aboard the USS *Kitty Hawk* in 1966, by which time a second squadron, VAW-12, had also been formed. Sixty-two E-2As were built, including the prototypes, and construction ended early in 1967. The E-2B, which flew in February 1969, had a number of refinements including an

A Grumman E-2C Hawkeye prepares for catapult launch from a US carrier.

L-304 micro-electronic computer, and all operational E-2As were later updated to E-2B standard. The early model Hawkeyes were equipped with the General Electric APS-96 search and tracking radar, which even in its original form was capable of automatic target detection and tracking over water. Trials and modifications to reject unwanted ground signals resulted in a new radar, the APS-120, which was capable of target detection and tracking over both sea and land. The system was fitted in a new model, the E-2C. Two derivatives of the E-2C were the TE-2C trainer and the C-2A Greyhound carrier on-board delivery transport.

Grumman E-2C Hawkeye

Type:	airborne command and control/AEW aircraft with five crew
Powerplant:	two 3020kW (4050hp) Allison T56-A-8A turboprops
Performance:	maximum speed 595km/h (370mph); service ceiling 9660m (31,700ft); range 3060km (1900 miles)
Weights:	empty 17,859kg (39,379lb); maximum take-off 22,453kg (49,500lb)
Dimensions:	wing span 24.56m (80ft 7in); length 17.17m (56ft 4in); height 5.58m (18ft 4in)
Armament:	none

The Hawkeye has been constantly upgraded throughout its long career with the US Navy, dating back to 1964.

A beautiful picture of three F-14A Tomcat aircraft of Fighter Squadron VF-2.

Having won a US Navy contest for a carrier-borne fighter to replace the Phantom in January 1969, the prototype F-14A first flew on 21 December 1970. The fighter completed carrier trials in the summer of 1972 and deliveries to the US Navy began in October that year. At the heart of the Tomcat's offensive capability is the Hughes AN/AWG-9 weapons control system, which enables the two-man crew to detect airborne targets at ranges of up to 315km (195 miles), depending on their size, and cruise missiles at 120km (75 miles). The system can track 24 targets and initiate attacks on six of them at the same time, at a variety of altitudes and ranges. 478 aircraft were supplied to the US Navy in total, and 80 more F-14As were exported to Iran in the later 1970s. The F-14D is an improved version with more powerful radar, enhanced avionics, a redesigned cockpit and a tactical jamming system. The Tomcat saw action in the Iran/Iraq war, the Gulf War, the Balkans and Afghanistan, and in the 1980s was involved in several clashes with Libyan fighters over the Gulf of Sirte.

Grumman F-14A Tomcat

Type:	two-seat fleet defence interceptor
Powerplant:	two 9480kg (20,900lb) thrust Pratt & Whitney TF30-P-412A turbofans
Performance:	maximum speed 2517km/h (1564mph) at altitude; service ceiling 17,070m (56,000ft); combat range 1994km (1239 miles)
Weights:	Empty 18,191kg (40,104lb); maximum take-off 33,724kg (74,349lb)
Dimensions:	wing span 19.55m (64ft 1.5in) unswept, 11.65m (38ft 2.5in) swept; length 19.1m (62ft 8in); height: 4.88m (16ft)
Armament:	one 20mm (0.79in) Vulcan rotary cannon, plus a variety of AAMs

An F-14 Tomcat pictured during a high-speed run, with wings fully swept back.

UNITED STATES

LOCKHEED F-104G STARFIGHTER

Development of the F-104 began in 1951, when the lessons of the Korean air war were starting to bring about profound changes in combat aircraft design. A contract for two XF-104 prototypes was placed in 1953 and the first of these flew on 7 February 1954, only 11 months later.

German Navy Starfighters received a dark grey upper surface camouflage, rendering them almost invisible against the Baltic at low level. The orange patches on the tanks were a safety measure, and would have been removed for combat sorties.

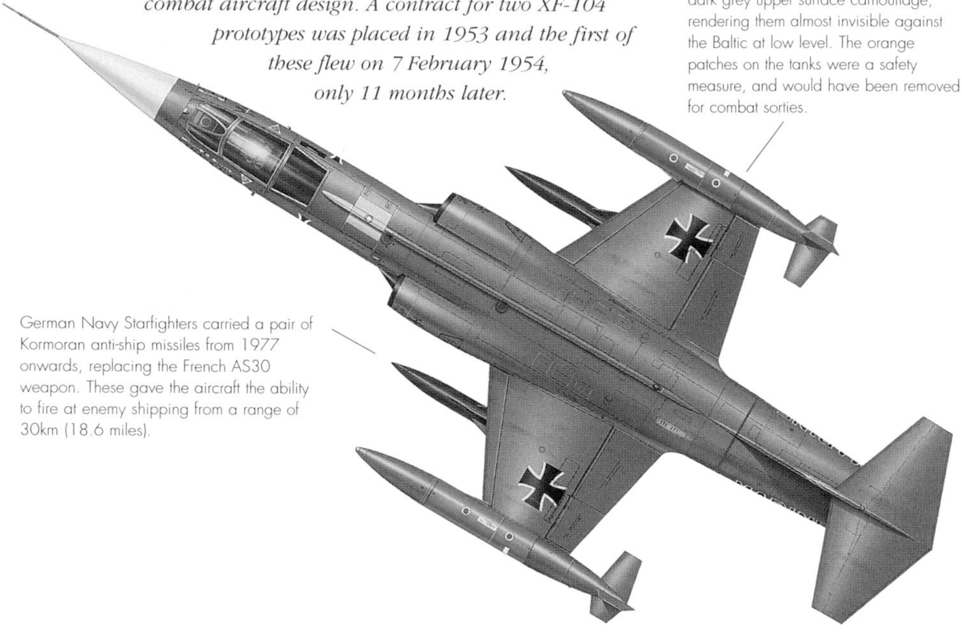

German Navy Starfighters carried a pair of Kormoran anti-ship missiles from 1977 onwards, replacing the French AS30 weapon. These gave the aircraft the ability to fire at enemy shipping from a range of 30km (18.6 miles).

The F-104G pictured here served until 1982 with Marineflieger Geschwader MFG.1, based at Schleswig in northern Germany. Federal Germany, Italy and Norway were the only operators of the Starfighter in the anti-shipping role. The German Navy received a total of 119 F-104Gs and 27 RF-104Gs. The last Starfighters were retired in 1988, having been replaced by the Panavia Tornado.

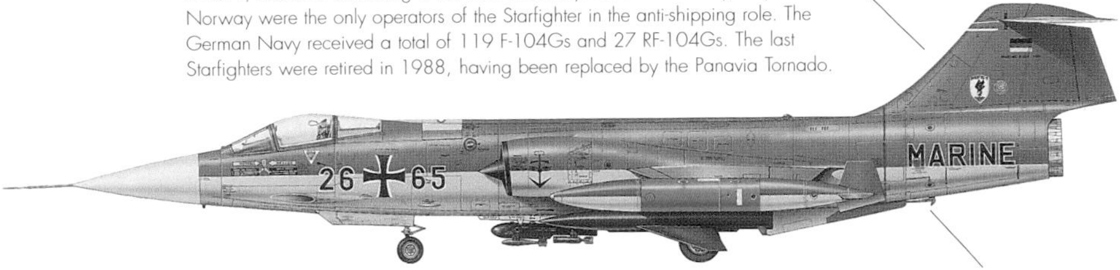

European-built Starfighters were fitted with a field arrester hook, which could be deployed to stop the aircraft running off the end of the runway in an emergency.

The Starfighter featured an ultra-thin, short-span wing with a leading-edge sweep of 26 degrees. Felt strips could be added to the wing on the ground to prevent technicians from injuring themselves on the sharp leading edges.

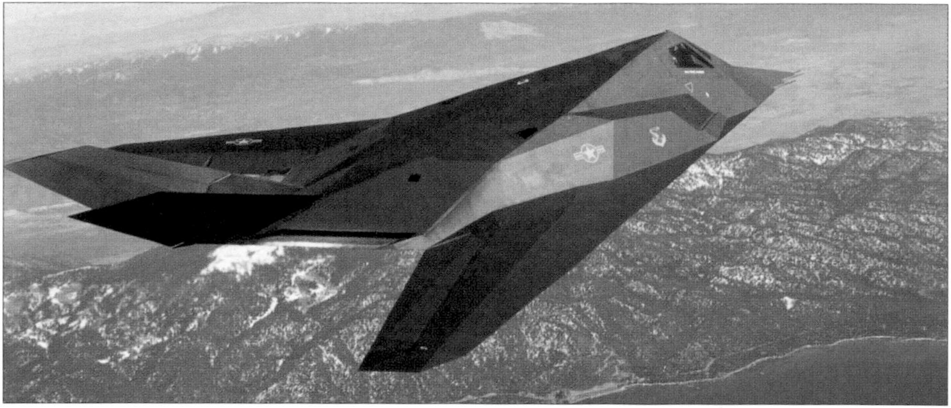

Two Experimental Stealth Tactical 'Have Blue' research aircraft were flown for the first time in 1977 at Groom Lake, Nevada (Area 51). One was destroyed in an accident, but the other completed the test programme successfully, leading to an order for 65 production F-117As. The aircraft made its first flight in June 1981 and entered service in October 1983. The F-117A is a single-seat, subsonic aircraft powered by two non-afterburning GE F404 turbofans with shielded slot exhausts designed to dissipate heat

The F-117A's development at Groom Lake, Nevada, was kept highly secret.

emissions (aided also by heat-shielding tiles), minimizing the infra red signature.The use of faceting (angled flat surfaces) scatters incoming radar energy; radar-absorbent materials and transparencies treated with conductive coating reduce the F-117A's radar signature still further. Armament is carried on swing-down trapezes in two internal bays. The F-117A has quadruple redundant fly-by-wire controls, head-up and head-down displays, laser communications and a nav/attack system. F-117As of the 37th Tactical Fighter Wing played a prominent part in the 1991 Gulf War, and have since been used in the Balkans and Afghanistan.

Lockheed F-117A Night Hawk

Type: single-seat stealth interdictor

Powerplant: two 4899kg (10,800lb) thrust General Electric F404-GE-F1D2 turbofans.

Performance: maximum speed 0.92M at altitude; service ceiling classified; range classified

Weights: empty approx 13,608kg (30,000lb); maximum take-off 23,814kg (52,500lb)

Dimensions: wing span 13.2m (43ft 4in), length 20.08m (65ft 11in); height 3.78m (12ft 5in)

Armament: provision for 2268kg (5000lb) of munitions on rotary dispenser in weapons bay, including a variety of missiles and bombs

The profile of the F-117A Night Hawk helps to reduce its radar signature.

UNITED STATES

UNITED STATES

Lockheed Martin F-16D Fighting Falcon

One of military aviation's big success stories, the F-16, designed and built by General Dynamics, had its origin in a USAF requirement of 1972 for a lightweight fighter and first flew on 2 February 1974.

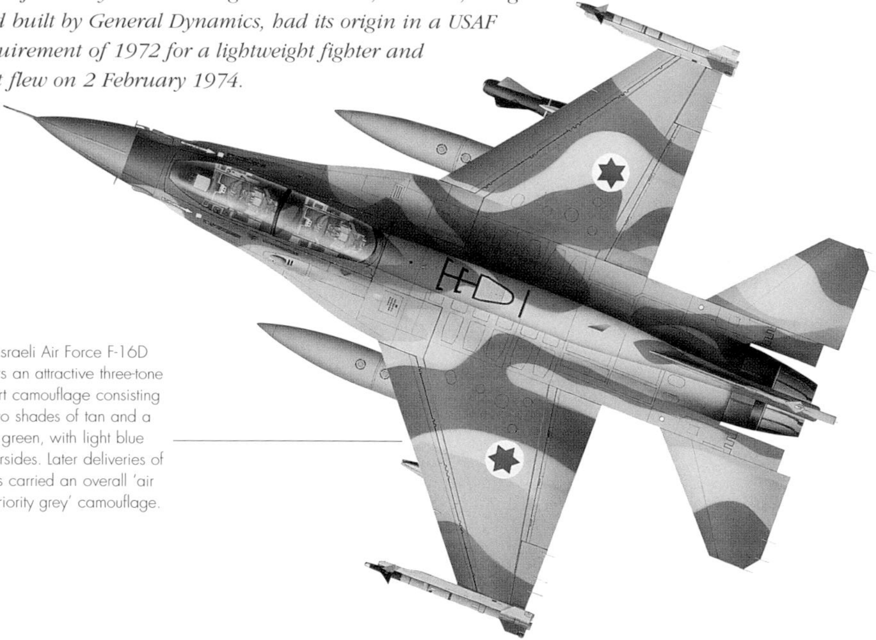

This Israeli Air Force F-16D wears an attractive three-tone desert camouflage consisting of two shades of tan and a pale green, with light blue undersides. Later deliveries of F-16s carried an overall 'air superiority grey' camouflage.

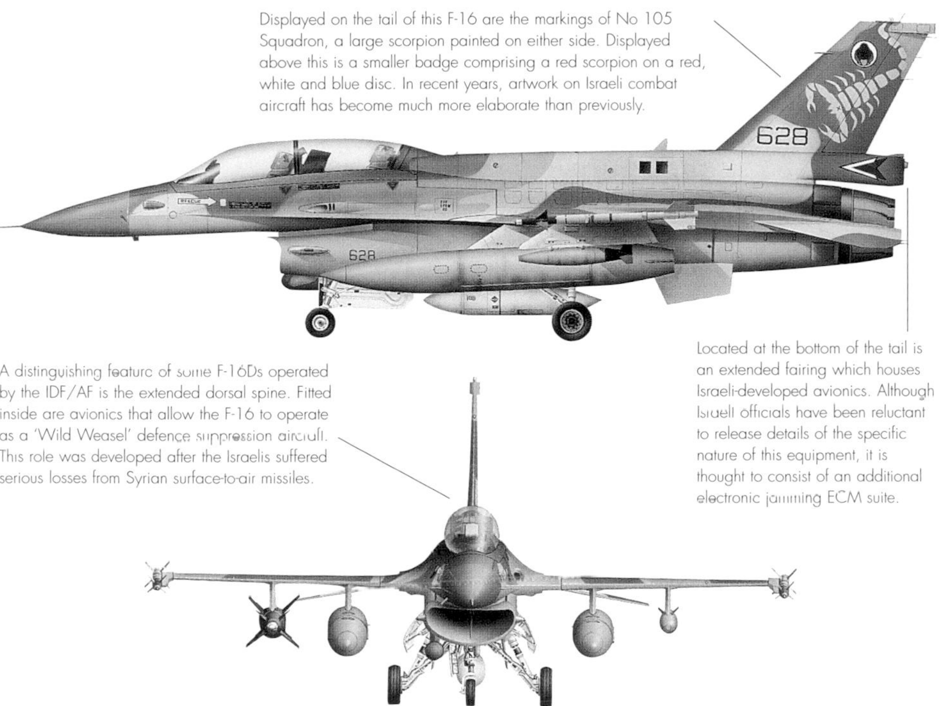

Displayed on the tail of this F-16 are the markings of No 105 Squadron, a large scorpion painted on either side. Displayed above this is a smaller badge comprising a red scorpion on a red, white and blue disc. In recent years, artwork on Israeli combat aircraft has become much more elaborate than previously.

A distinguishing feature of some F-16Ds operated by the IDF/AF is the extended dorsal spine. Fitted inside are avionics that allow the F-16 to operate as a 'Wild Weasel' defence suppression aircraft. This role was developed after the Israelis suffered serious losses from Syrian surface-to-air missiles.

Located at the bottom of the tail is an extended fairing which houses Israeli-developed avionics. Although Israeli officials have been reluctant to release details of the specific nature of this equipment, it is thought to consist of an additional electronic jamming ECM suite.

In service with many air arms other than the USAF, the F-16 carries an advanced GEC-Marconi HUDWACS (Head-Up Display and Weapon Aiming Computer System). The HUDWAC computer is used to direct the weapons to the target, as designated on the HUD. The F-16 HUDWAC shows horizontal and vertical speed, altitude, heading, climb and roll bars and range-to-go information. There are five ground-attack modes and four air combat modes. In air combat, the 'snapshoot' mode lets the pilot aim at crossing targets by drawing a

Seen here is a 'Block 50D' aircraft, first delivered to the USAF in May 1993.

continuously computed impact line (CCIL) on the HUD. The lead-computing off sight (LCOS) mode follows a designated target; the dogfight mode combines snapshoot and LCOS; and there is also an air-to-air missile mode. The F-16B and -D were two-seat versions, and the F-16C (delivered from 1988) incorporated improved avionics and came with a choice of engines. F-16s have seen action in the Lebanon (with the Israeli Air Force), in the Gulf War and the Balkans. The aircraft has been constantly upgraded to extend its life well into the 21st century.

Lockheed Martin F-16D

Type:	two-seat air superiority and strike fighter
Powerplant:	one 13,150kg (28,990lb) thrust General Electric F110-GE-100 turbofan
Performance:	maximum speed 2142km/h (1330mph) at altitude; service ceiling 15,240m (50,000ft); combat radius 925km (575 miles)
Weights:	empty 7070kg (15,586lb); maximum take-off 16,057kg (35,400lb)
Dimensions:	wing span 9.45m (31ft); length 15.09m (49ft 6in); height 5.09m (16ft 8in)
Armament:	one M61A1 multi-barrelled cannon; seven hardpoints for up to 9276kg (20,450lb) of ordnance

The F-16 is a popular aircraft, proven to be very reliable and adaptable.

In the late 1970s the USAF identified a requirement for 750 Advanced Tactical Fighters (ATF) to replace the F-15 Eagle. In September 1983, the USAF awarded ATF study contracts to six American aerospace companies and of these, two (Lockheed and Northrop) were selected to build demonstrator prototypes of their respective proposals. In April 1991 the USAF announced that the winning combination was the Lockheed F-22, with the Pratt & Whitney advanced technology engine F119. The F-22 combines many stealth features. Its air-to-air

The F-22's innovative design includes the latest advances in aviation technology.

weapons, for example, are stored internally; three internal bays house advanced short-range, medium-range and beyond visual range air-to-air missiles. Following an assessment of the aircraft's combat role in 1993, it was decided to add a ground-attack capability.The F-22 was designed to meet the threat presented in the early 1980s by large numbers of highly agile Soviet combat aircraft, its task being to engage them in their own airspace with beyond visual range weaponry.The first production F-22A flew on 7 September 1997. The USAF requirement is for 438 aircraft.

Lockheed Martin F-22A

Type:	single-seat air superiority fighter
Powerplant:	two 15,876kg (35,000lb) thrust Pratt & Whitney F119-P-100 turbofans
Performance:	maximum speed 2335km/h (1450mph) at altitude; service ceiling 19,812m (65,000ft); combat radius 1285km (800 miles)
Weights:	empty 14,062kg (31,000lb); maximum take-off 27,216kg (60,000lb)
Dimensions:	wing span 13.1m (43ft); length 19.55m (64ft 2in); height 5.39m (17ft 8in)
Armament:	AAMs and other advanced weapons

The expense of developing the F-22 is rivalled only by that of the B-2 bomber.

UNITED STATES

LOCKHEED (LOCKHEED MARTIN) P-3 ORION

The first of two YP3V-1 prototypes flew on 19 August 1958 and deliveries of production P-3As began in August 1962. Total P-3A/B production ran to 286 aircraft for the US Navy, plus five for the RNZAF, ten for the RAAF, and five for Norway. The P-3C, which appeared in 1969, was equipped with a Univac digital

The Lockheed P-3 Orion was developed from the Lockheed Electra civil airliner.

computer, the nerve centre of a fully integrated search, analysis and attack system. Further improvements were incorporated in 1974–75, and in addition to the 132 P-3Cs delivered to the USN, ten aircraft were ordered by the RAF. Further variants of the Orion include the EP-3A electronic intelligence aircraft, the P-3F, six of which were delivered to the Imperial Iranian Air Force in 1975, and the CP-140 Aurora for the Canadian Armed Forces. The Orion was built under licence in Japan (100 aircraft), and also serves in Australia, the Republic of Korea, the Netherlands, Pakistan, Portugal and Spain. The aircraft has been continually upgraded in US Navy service. At the time of writing, Lockheed Martin and Raytheon are working on a new series of patrol aircraft based on an updated Orion airframe.

Lockheed P-3C Orion

Type:	long-range maritime patrol aircraft with 10 crew
Powerplant:	four 3661kW (4910hp) Allison T56-A-14 turboprops
Performance:	maximum speed 761km/h (473mph) at 4570m (15,000ft); service ceiling 8625m (28,300ft); range: 3835km (2383 miles)
Weights:	empty 27,982kg (61,700lb); maximum take-off 64,410kg (142,000lb)
Dimensions:	wing span 30.37m (99ft 8in); length 35.61m (116ft 10in); height 10.29m (33ft 9in)
Armament:	up to 8735kg (19,250lb) of ASW munitions

The Orion has a good export record, having been supplied to many countries.

UNITED STATES

Lockheed S-3B Viking

Although it began life as a dedicated ASW platform, the extremely versatile Lockheed S-3 Viking has undertaken other roles, including tanking, mining and limited electronic surveillance.

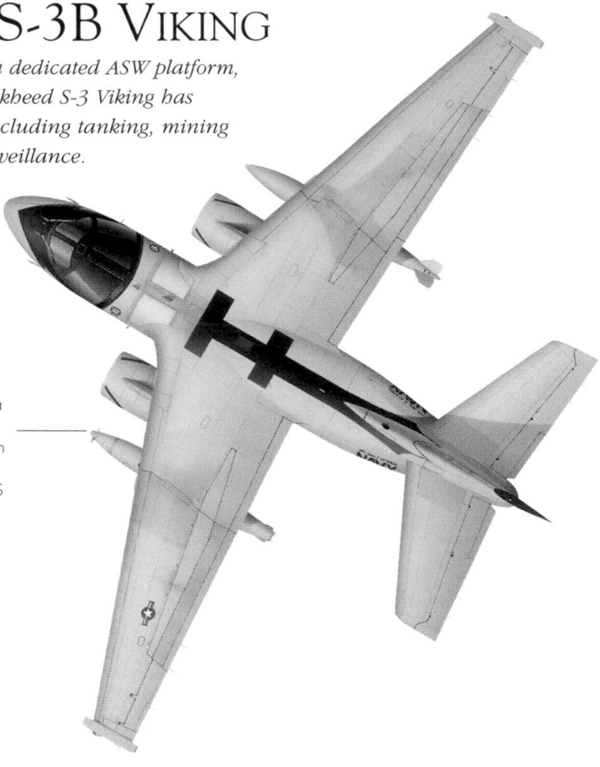

A typical flexible mission load consists of one AGM-84D (Block 1C) Harpoon anti-ship missile and a refuelling pod, with two Mk 82 bombs and two Mk 46 torpedoes in the aircraft's weapons bays. This aircraft carries a 1136-litre (300 US gal) drop tank in place of the Harpoon.

For most of its career, the Viking flew with a crew of four in the ASW role, comprising two pilots, a Tactical Co-ordinator (Tacco) and an enlisted sensor operator (Senso). Aircraft converted as permanent tankers have a two-man crew – the pilot and a naval flight officer.

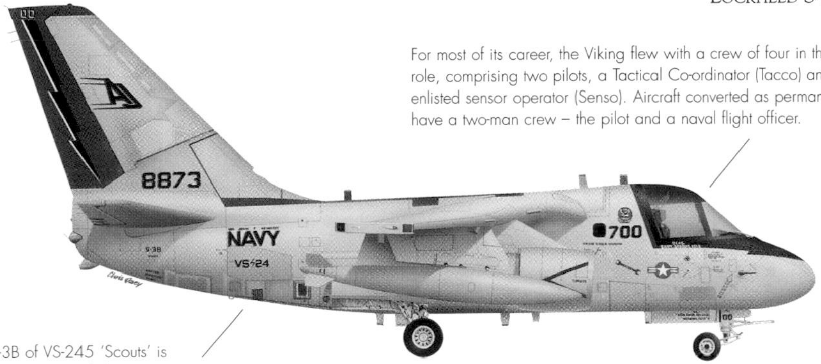

This S-3B of VS-245 'Scouts' is seen as it appeared during its 1997 cruise aboard the carrier USS *John F. Kennedy* (CV-67) as part of Carrier Air Wing Eight. VS-24 was the first unit to deploy the S-3B in combat, during the 1991 Operation Desert Storm.

When fulfilling its tanker mission, the S-3B uses an ARS 31-301 'buddy' pod mounted on the left wing station. Almost all Viking missions are flown with the 'buddy' pod affixed. Internal fuel capacity totals 7190 litres (1900 US gal).

UNITED STATES

The Lockheed S-3 Viking was designed in response to a 1969 US Navy requirement for a carrier-borne ASW system built around a Univac digital computer. The prototype first flew on 21 January 1972, and 93 production SA-3As had been ordered by the end of 1973, deliveries beginning in March 1974. The last

The Lockheed S-3 Viking has proved an extremely adaptable aircraft.

of 187 Vikings was delivered to the USN in 1978. The Viking fleet was substantially updated to S-3B standard in the early 1990s, some aircraft being converted to the electronic warfare role as ES-3As. The S-3B's high-speed computer system processes information from the acoustic and non-acoustic target sensor systems; these include new Inverse Synthetic Aperture radar (ISAR) and ESM systems suites. To engage its targets, the S-3B employs an impressive array of airborne weaponry. This provides the fleet with a very effective airborne capability to combat the significant threat posed by modern surface combatants and submarines, although the Viking's ASW role was dropped in 1998. In addition, all S-3B aircraft can carry an inflight refuelling 'buddy' store, allowing the transfer of fuel from the Viking to other naval strike aircraft, extending their combat radius.

Lockheed (Lockheed Martin) S-3B Viking

Type:	carrier-borne multi-purpose aircraft with four crew
Powerplant:	two 4207kg (9275lb) thrust General Electric TF34-GE-400B turbofans
Performance:	maximum speed 828km/h (518mph); service ceiling: 12,200m (40,000ft); range 3705km (2302 miles)
Weights:	empty 12,088kg (26,650lb); maximum take off 19,278kg (42,500lb)
Dimensions:	wing span 20.93m (68ft 8in); length 16.26m (53ft 4in); height 6.93m (22ft 9in)
Armament:	provision for up to 1794kg (3958lb) of munitions

An S-3 Viking armed with Harpoon anti-ship missiles.

Work on the SR-71 began in 1959, when a Lockheed team embarked on the design of a radical new aircraft to supersede the Lockheed U-2 in the strategic reconnaissance role. Designated A-12, the new machine took shape in conditions of great secrecy in the restricted section of the Lockheed Burbank plant (the 'Skunk Works') and seven aircraft were produced by the summer of 1964. Early flight tests were aimed at assessing the A-12's suitability as a long-range interceptor, and the experimental interceptor version was shown

The Lockheed SR-71A brought a new dimension to strategic reconnaissance.

to the public at Edwards AFB in September 1964, bearing the designation YF-12A. Plans to build the interceptor were abandoned, but work on the SR-71 reconnaissance variant continued, and the prototype flew for the first time on 22 December 1964. Twenty aircraft were built, deliveries beginning to the 4200th Strategic Reconnaissance Wing in January 1966. The SR-71A's main operating unit was the 9th SRW, which deployed detachments of SR-71As worldwide, as required. The SR-71 gave the USAF an unparalleled strategic reconnaissance capability. Its high speed and altitude made it possible for the aircraft to penetrate hostile airspace with virtual impunity.

Lockheed SR-71A

Type:	two-seat strategic reconnaissance aircraft
Powerplant:	two 14,742kg (32,500lb) Pratt & Whitney JT11D-20B turbojets
Performance:	maximum speed 3220km/h (2000mph) at 24,385m (80,000ft); service ceiling 24,385m (80,000ft); range 4800km (2983 miles)
Weights:	empty 27,216kg (60,000lb); maximum take-off 77,111kg (170,000lb)
Dimensions:	wing span 16.94m (55ft 7in); length 32.74m (107ft 5in); height 5.64m (18ft 6in)
Armament:	none

A Lockheed SR-71A of the 9th Strategic Reconnaissance Wing being made ready for flight.

UNITED STATES

McDonnell Douglas AH-64 Apache

In January 1991, US AH-64 Apache helicopters began Operation Desert Storm by delivering a devastating attack on forward elements of the Iraqi air defence system. Since then, the Apache has proved its worth time and again.

Wire cutters are located forward of the nose turret, below the rotor hub, in front of the gun and on both main landing gear legs. These have proved highly effective when operating over urban areas.

The Apache can carry removable 30-round M130 chaff dispensers on a mounting to the rear of the tail boom, to starboard. The M130 can fire M1 chaff cartridges to defeat radar-guided weapons.

Israel has been an AH-64 operator since September 1990, and paints its Apaches in an IR-suppressive olive drab finish. For operations in the southern Lebanon, aircraft carry an IR-reflective 'V' identification marking on the rear fuselage.

The Apache's main landing gear has shock struts to absorb impact and a kneeling facility to allow for air transportation. Each landing strut has a one-time, high-impact absorbing capability, so reducing injury to the crew in the event of a forced landing.

The Apache's weapons pylons are articulated to provide the desired elevation for various fire control modes and for aerodynamic/handling purposes. When an Apache lands, the pylons automatically translate to ground stow mode, so that they are parallel with level terrain.

UNITED STATES

McDonnell Douglas F-4EJ Phantom II

One of the most potent and versatile combat aircraft ever built, the McDonnell F-4 Phantom stemmed from a 1954 project for an advanced naval fighter.

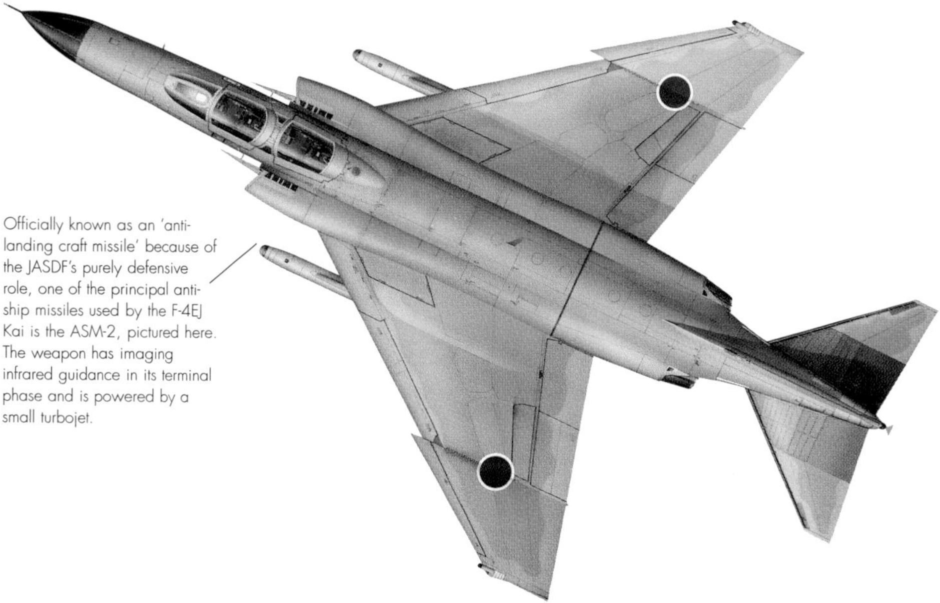

Officially known as an 'anti-landing craft missile' because of the JASDF's purely defensive role, one of the principal anti-ship missiles used by the F-4EJ Kai is the ASM-2, pictured here. The weapon has imaging infrared guidance in its terminal phase and is powered by a small turbojet.

The F-4E Phantom was used in large numbers by the Japanese Air Self-Defence Force, the F-4EJ being the licence-built version. Of the 140 F-4EJs procured, about two-thirds were upgraded to F-4EJ Kai standard with improved weapons and avionics systems, the Kai suffix denoting 'modified'.

External additions to the Kai-modified aircraft include twin aft-facing radar warning receivers on the tip of the tail fin, similar forward-facing antennae on the wingtips, and a large blade aerial mounted mid-spine for the new UHF radio.

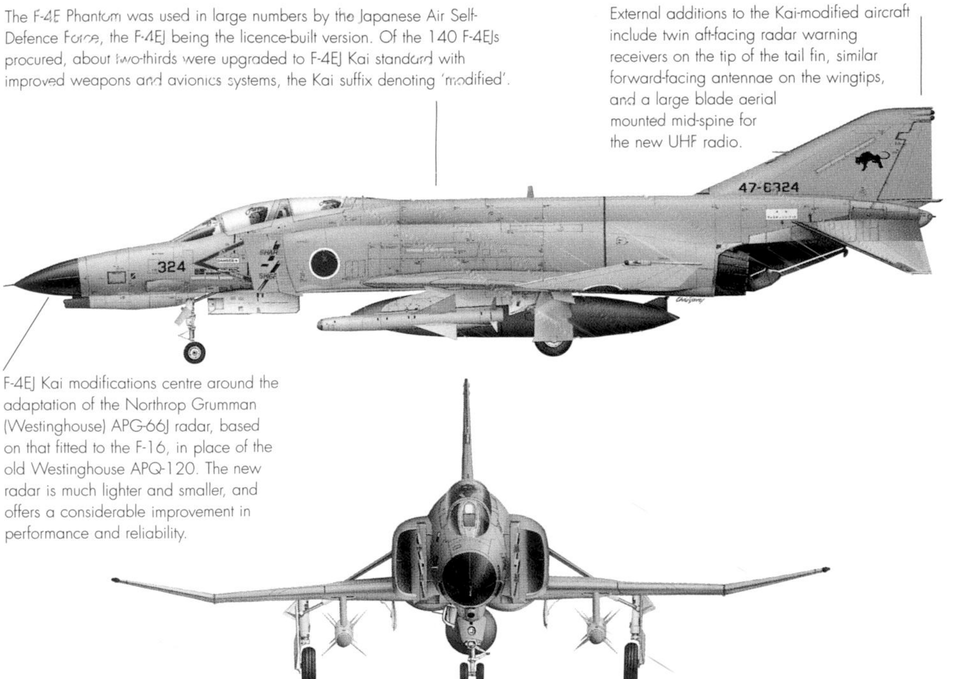

F-4EJ Kai modifications centre around the adaptation of the Northrop Grumman (Westinghouse) APG-66J radar, based on that fitted to the F-16, in place of the old Westinghouse APQ-120. The new radar is much lighter and smaller, and offers a considerable improvement in performance and reliability.

A McDonnell F-4E Phantom unleashes its load of 'iron bombs'.

The XF4H-1 prototype flew for the first time on 27 May 1958. Production Phantoms were originally designated F4H-1F, but this was later changed to F-4A. The F-4B was a slightly improved version with J79-GE-8 engines. Carrier trials were carried out in 1960, and the first Phantoms were delivered in December that year. A production order was soon placed for a USAF variant, the F-4C. The RF-4B and RF-4C were unarmed reconnaissance variants for the USMC and USAF, while the F-4D was basically an F-4C with improved systems and redesigned radome. The F-4E was the major production version. The RF-4E was a tactical reconnaissance variant. The F-4F (175 built) was a version for the Luftwaffe, while the F-4G Wild Weasel was the F4E modified for the suppression of enemy defence systems. The successor to the F-4B in USN/USMC service was the F-4J, which possessed greater ground-attack capability. Phantoms served with the air forces of Great Britain, Iran, Israel, Spain, Greece Japan, Turkey, South Korea and Australia, and the type saw combat in many parts of the world, notably Vietnam and the Middle East.

McDonnell F-4E Phantom II

Type:	two-seat fighter/attack aircraft
Powerplant:	two 8119kg (17,900lb) thrust General Electric J79-GE-17 turbojets
Performance:	maximum speed 2390km/h (1485mph) at altitude; service ceiling 18,975m (62,250ft); range 2817km (1750 miles)
Weights:	empty 12,700kg (28,000lb); maximum take-off 26,309kg (58,000lb)
Dimensions:	wing span 11.70m (38ft 5in); length 17.76m (58ft 3in); height 4.96m (16ft 3in)
Armament:	one 20mm (0.79in) cannon and four AAMs; up to 5888kg (12,980lb) of ordnance

An F-4E of the 4th Tactical Fighter Wing pictured at Seymour-Johnson Air Force Base, North Carolina.

This F-15C was used as a test aircraft for the LANTIRN radar system.

In 1969 it was announced that McDonnell Douglas had been selected as prime airframe contractor for a new air superiority fighter, designated FX. As the F-15A Eagle, it flew for the first time on 27 July 1972, and first deliveries of operational aircraft were made to the USAF in 1975. The F-15 Eagle was designed to outfly and outfight any opponent it might encounter, in engagements extending from beyond visual range right down to close-in turning combat. The tandem-seat F-15B was developed alongside the F-15A, and the main production version was the F-15C (built under licence in Japan as the F-15J). The F-15E Strike Eagle is a dedicated strike/attack variant and, while the F-15C established and maintained air superiority, carried out precision bombing operations in the 1991 Gulf War. The F-15E was supplied to Israel as the F-15I and to Saudi Arabia as the F-15S. In all, the USAF took delivery of 1286 F-15s (all versions), Japan 171, Saudi Arabia 98 and Israel 56. Apart from action in the Gulf War, Israeli aircraft were in combat with the Syrian Air Force over the Bekaa Valley in the 1980s.

McDonnell Douglas F-15C Eagle

Type:	single-seat air superiority fighter
Powerplant:	two 10,800kg (23,810lb) thrust Pratt & Whitney F100-PW-220 turbofans
Performance:	maximum speed 2655km/h (1650mph) at altitude; service ceiling 30,500m (100,000ft); range 1930km (1200 miles) on internal fuel
Weights:	empty 12,970kg (28,600lb); maximum take-off 30,845kg (68,000lb)
Dimensions:	wing span 13.05m (42ft 9.67in); length 19.43m (63ft 9in); height 5.63m (18ft 5in)
Armament:	one 20mm (0.79in) cannon; eight AAMs; up to 7620kg (16,800lb) of munitions

This F-15C is based in Spain, as part of NATO's Mediterranean air defences.

UNITED STATES

McDonnell Douglas F/A-18D Hornet

While the F-14 replaced the Phantom in the naval air superiority role, the aircraft that replaced it in the tactical role (with both the USN and USMC) was the McDonnell Douglas F-18 Hornet.

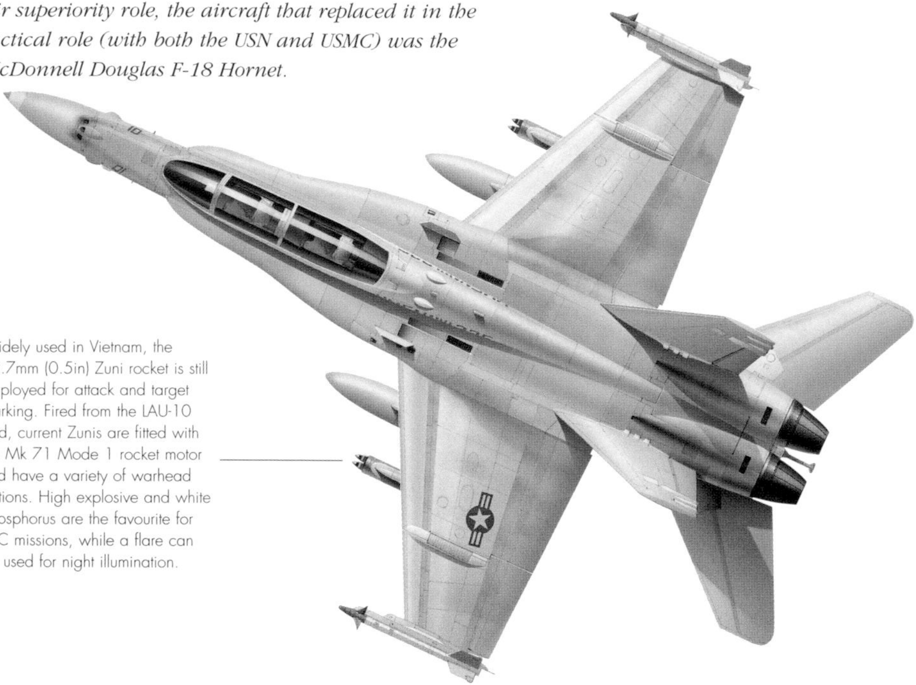

Widely used in Vietnam, the 12.7mm (0.5in) Zuni rocket is still employed for attack and target marking. Fired from the LAU-10 pod, current Zunis are fitted with the Mk 71 Mode 1 rocket motor and have a variety of warhead options. High explosive and white phosphorus are the favourite for FAC missions, while a flare can be used for night illumination.

The F/A-18D inherited the precision attack role from the Grumman A-6 Intruder, and the job of the Hornet's second crew member is to operate the sophisticated avionics/sensor suite. Whereas most two-seat Hornets are used for training, those of the USMC are optimized for an offensive role, with no flight controls in the back seat but full weapon system controls instead.

One role for the Hornet is that of fast forward air control, the backseater controlling other aircraft over the battlefield. Targets are marked with rockets carried in four-round pods under the wings, while the aircraft carries a forward-looking infrared and laser spot tracker on the intake pylons.

The Martin-Marietta ASQ-173 pod on the port intake contains a laser spot tracker in the nose for attacking targets designated by other sources, and a strike camera in the rear section for rapid damage assessment.

Two US Marine Corps F/A-18s pictured during a training exercise over Nevada.

First flown on 18 November 1978, the prototype Hornet was followed by 11 development aircraft. The first production versions were the fighter/attack F/A-18A and the two-seat F/A-18B operational trainer; subsequent variants were the F/A-18C and F/A-18D, which had provision for AIM-120 AAMs and Maverick infra red missiles as well as an airborne self-protection jamming system. The two-seat F/A-18D was equipped with the Advanced Tactical Airborne Reconnaissance System (ATARS) and replaced the RF-4 Phantom in service with the US Marine Corps; this version first saw combat duty in Kosovo in May 1999. The aircraft also serves with the Canadian Armed Forces as the CF-18 (138 aircraft). Other customers are Australia (75), Finland (64), Kuwait (40), Malaysia (8), Spain (72) and Switzerland (34). Total US deliveries, all variants, were 1150 aircraft. The Hornet's exceptional record and its suitability for continuous upgrading have stimulated continued international interest, with the Philippines, Chile, the Czech Republic, Hungary and Poland all potential customers.

McDonnell Douglas F/A-18D Hornet

Type:	two-seat fighter and strike aircraft
Powerplant:	two 7264kg (16,000lb) thrust General Electric F404-GE-400 turbofans
Performance:	maximum speed 1912km/h (1183mph) at 12,190m (40,000ft); service ceiling 15,240m (50,000ft); combat radius 1020km (634 miles)
Weights:	empty 10,455kg (23,050lb); maximum take-off 25,401kg (56,000lb)
Dimensions:	wing span 11.43m (37ft 6in); length 17.07m (56ft); height 4.66m (15ft 3.5in)
Armament:	one 20mm (0.79in) cannon; up to 7711kg (17,000lb) of munitions

A US Marine Corps two-seat F/A-18D of VMA(AW)-533 practises a bombing run.

UNITED STATES

A pair of AV-8B Harrier IIs of Marine Corps Squadron VMA-211 'Avengers'.

Although it was the British who were responsible for the early design and development of this remarkable aircraft, albeit with much American funding, it was the US Marine Corps who identified the need to upgrade their original version, the AV-8A. The Harrier used 1950s technology in its airframe and systems, and by the 1970s, despite systems updates, this was restricting further development of the aircraft's potential. The basic design concept was retained in the USMC's new Harrier variant, but new technologies and avionics were fully exploited. One of the major improvements was a new wing, with a carbon fibre composite structure, a super-critical aerofoil, and a greater area and span. A prototype AV-8B Harrier II first flew in November 1978, followed by the first development aircraft in November 1981, and production deliveries to the USMC began in 1983. Delivery of the RAF's equivalent, the Harrier GR5, began in 1987; production GR5s were later converted to GR7 standard. This version, similar to the USMC's night-attack AV-8B, has FLIR, a digital moving map display, night vision goggles for the pilot and a modified head-up display.

McDD/BAe AV-8B Harrier II

Type:	single-seat V/STOL close support aircraft
Powerplant:	one 10,796kg (23,800lb) thrust Rolls-Royce F402-RR-408 vectored thrust turbofan
Performance:	maximum speed 1065km/h (661mph); service ceiling 15,240m (50,000ft); combat radius 277km (172 miles) with 2722kg (6000lb) payload
Weights:	empty 5936kg (13,086lb); maximum take-off 14,061kg (31,000lb)
Dimensions:	wing span 9.25m (30ft 4in); length 14.12m (46ft 4in); height 3.55m (11ft 7.67in)
Armament:	one 25mm (0.984in) cannon; up to 7711kg (17,000lb) of munitions

An AV-8B Night Attack Harrier armed with Maverick air-to-surface missiles.

Two Canadian Armed Forces CF-101Bs over their home base.

The resurrected XF-88 design was subjected to a number of changes, including the lengthening of the fuselage by over 4.00m (13ft) to accommodate extra fuel tankage, and the remodelled aircraft was designated YF-101A. The prototype flew on 29 December 1954, and although Strategic Air Command had long since abandoned the long-range escort fighter idea, the programme was taken over by Tactical Air Command, which saw the F-101 as a potential replacement for the Northrop F-89 Scorpion. The aircraft went into production as the F-101A, and the 75 built equipped three squadrons of TAC. The next Voodoo variant, the two-seat F-101B, equipped 16 squadrons of Air Defense Command, and production ran to 359 aircraft. This version also equipped three Canadian air defence squadrons as the CF-101B. The F-101C was a single-seat fighter-bomber version, entering service with the 523rd Tactical Fighter Squadron of the 27th Fighter Bomber Wing in May 1957. It equipped nine squadrons, but its operational career was short-lived, being replaced by more modern combat types in the early 1960s.

McDonnell F-101B Voodoo

Type:	two-seat all-weather long-range interceptor
Powerplant:	two 7672kg (16,900lb) thrust Pratt & Whitney J57-P-55 turbojets
Performance:	maximum speed 1965km/h (1221mph) at 12,190m (40,000ft); service ceiling 16,705m (54,800ft); range 2494km (1550 miles)
Weights:	empty 13,141kg (28,970lb); maximum take-off 23,768kg (52,400lb)
Dimensions:	wing span 12.09m (39ft 8in); length 20.54m (67ft 4.67in); height 5.49m (18ft))
Armament:	two nuclear tipped and four conventional AAMs

Two F-101Bs of the USAF Air Defense Command patrol during the Cold War.

UNITED STATES

UNITED STATES

North American F-86E Sabre

Probably the best-known jet fighter of all, the North American F-86 Sabre earned its spurs in the Korean War, where it established a ten-to-one kill ratio over communist MiG-15s – most of which were flown by Russian pilots.

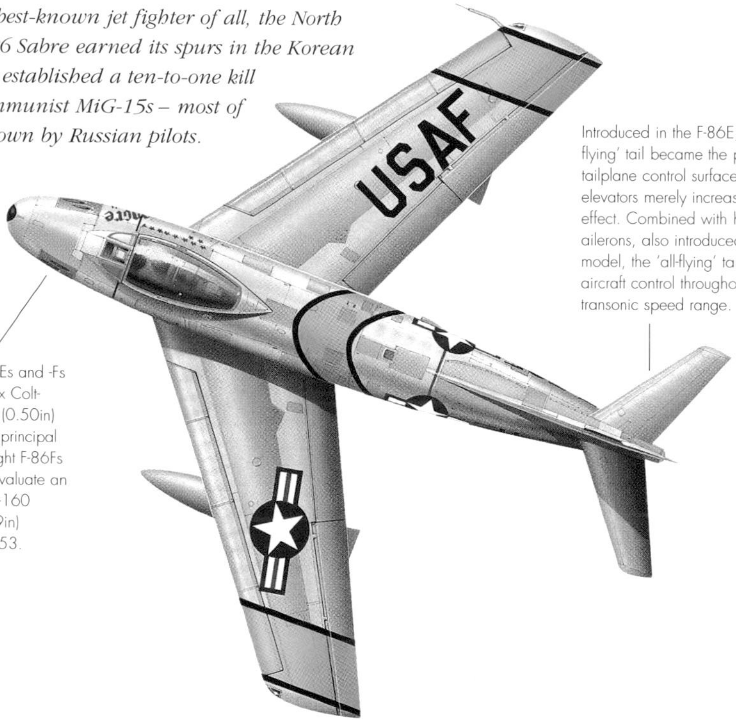

Introduced in the F-86E, the 'all-flying' tail became the primary tailplane control surface, the elevators merely increasing its effect. Combined with hydraulic ailerons, also introduced in the E-model, the 'all-flying' tail improved aircraft control throughout the transonic speed range.

Almost all F-86As, -Es and -Fs were armed with six Colt-Browning 12.7mm (0.50in) machine guns. The principal exceptions were eight F-86Fs that were used to evaluate an installation of four T-160 (M39) 20mm (0.79in) cannon in early 1953.

The F-86E-10 introduced a new, flat, armoured glass windscreen, which gave much improved forward protection and vision than compared with the earlier V-shaped unit.

Elenore 'E' was F-86E-10-NA 51-2735, flown by Major William T. Whisner if the 25th Fighter Intercepter Squadron, 51st Fighter Intercepter Wing. Bill Whisner scored 5½ kills in Korea, adding to the 15½ scored in World War II, when he flew P-47s and P-51s with the 487th Fighter Squadron.

Sabre operations in north-west Korea, known as 'MiG Alley', were hampered throughout the war by a shortage of underwing drop tanks, despite the fact that a tank production line was set up at Misawa in Japan.

UNITED STATES

Northrop T-38 Talon

First flown in April 1959, the Northrop T-38A Talon jet trainer stemmed from the same programme that produced the F-5 Freedom Fighter and was developed as a private venture over a period of two years.

The T-38's two General Electric J85-GE-6 engines, each producing 1746kg (3850lb) of thrust, provide advanced students with experience of both afterburning and twin-engine operation. One engine is sufficient to power the T-38 safely round an airfield circuit.

USAF

For many years, the USAF's T-38 fleet served in an all-white colour scheme, and indeed some still do so. However, the fleet is gradually adopting the smart blue/white scheme seen here, so that aircraft are more conspicuous in various weather conditions.

For advanced pilot training, a typical en route (cruising) speed and airfield pattern speed is 300 knots (553km/h; 344mph). Flying skills are taught through the full range of the aircraft's performance, although Mach 1 is normally only exceeded to give student pilots the experience of supersonic flight.

The T-38's landing gear is necessarily strong to handle the many landing cycles undertaken by training aircraft. In the event of systems failure, the landing gear extends and locks under gravity.

Three YF-38 prototypes were ordered, and after a further year of development, during which flight trials were undertaken to assess the performance of different powerplants, the aircraft entered USAF service in March 1961. Between 24 August and 12 October, 1961, the noted American pilot Jacqueline

Pilot and instructor perform checks on their T-38 Talon before take-off.

Cochran set up a series of international records for women pilots while flying a T-38. These included a speed of 1028.99km/h (640.3mph) over a 1000km closed circuit, a distance of 216.77km

(134.63 miles) in a closed circuit, an altitude of 17,091m (56,073ft) and a sustained altitude of 16,841m (55,253ft) over a 15/25km course. The T-38 was produced at the rate of 12 aircraft per month, the 500th being delivered on 30 November 1964. The aircraft proved highly successful, with 1139 eventually completed.

ASTRONAUT TRAINING

Some T-38s were used for astronaut training, being able to simulate negative gravity conditions in a pushover from a zoom climb, while others simulated MiG-21s in air combat

Northrop T-38A Talon

Type:	two-seat supersonic trainer
Powerplant:	two 1746kg (3850lb) General Electric J85-GE-6 turbojets
Performance:	maximum speed 1381km/h (858mph) at 10,975m (36,000ft); service ceiling 16,340m (53,600ft); range 1759km (1093 miles)
Weights:	empty 3254kg (7174lb); maximum take-off 5361kg (11,820lb)
Dimensions:	wing span 7.70m (25ft 3in); length 14.14m (46ft 4.5in); height 3.92m (12ft 10.5in)
Armament:	none

schools. The T-38 is still used by the USAF in various capacities in the early 21st century.

These T-38s show their graceful lines as they break away from the camera.

UNITED STATES

SIKORSKY MH-53J

The infiltration and extraction of special forces to and from enemy territory by air dates back to World War II. It was for this task that the US Air Force's 'Pave Low' programme was initiated, using helicopters.

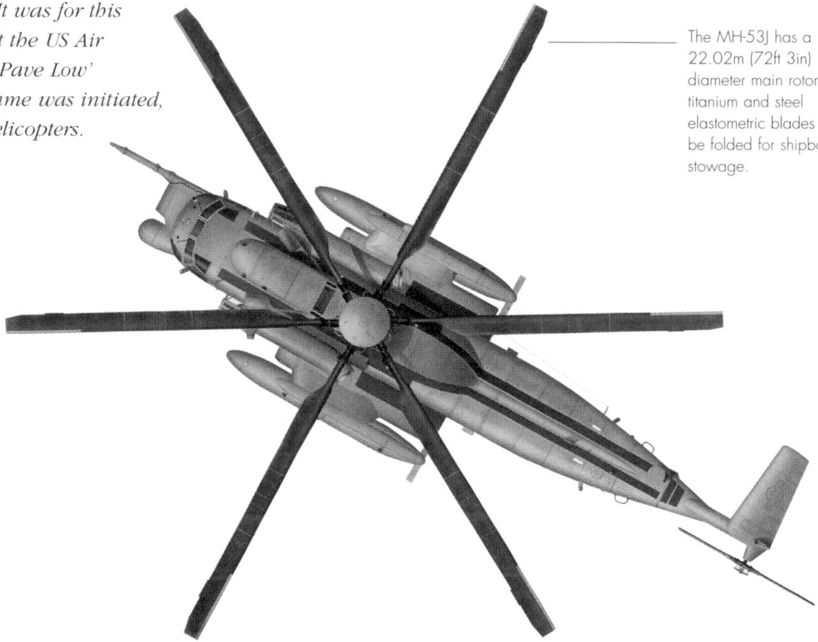

The MH-53J has a 22.02m (72ft 3in) diameter main rotor. The titanium and steel elastometric blades can be folded for shipboard stowage.

In 1997 the MH-53J seen here was based at RAF Mildenhall, Suffolk, with the 21st 'Dust Devils' Special Operations Squadron of the 352nd Special Operations Group. It has adopted the new low-IR signature overall grey finish in place of the green 'European One' camouflage worn previously.

The MH-53J Pave Low IIIE carries three 7.62mm (0.30in) rapid firing miniguns, two mounted on either side of the fuselage, and one mounted on the rear ramp. Three 12.7mm guns may be mounted as an alternative, or two 7.62s may be mounted in the side windows and one 12.7mm on the ramp. The 12.7mm has 450 rounds, some of which are armour-piercing.

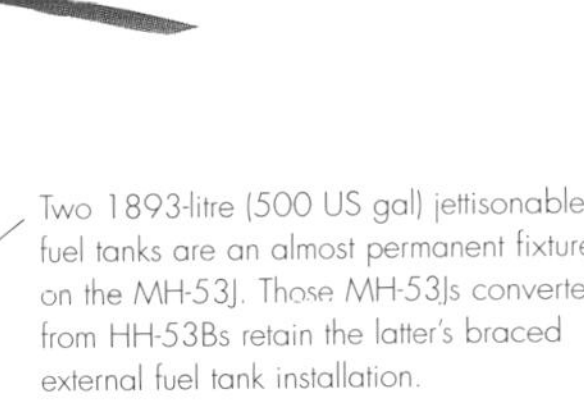

Two 1893-litre (500 US gal) jettisonable fuel tanks are an almost permanent fixture on the MH-53J. Those MH-53Js converted from HH-53Bs retain the latter's braced external fuel tank installation.

A Vought A-7E Corsair II of US Navy Attack Squadron VA-27, USS *Enterprise*.

Based on the design of the F-8 Crusader, the Corsair II was designed for high subsonic speed. This made it possible to reduce structural weight, increasing range and payload. Development was rapid, losses sustained by the A-4 Skyhawk squadrons in Vietnam making it imperative to bring the new aircraft into combat as quickly as possible. The prototype flew for the first time on 27 September 1965. The first attack variant was the A-7A, which made its combat debut in the Gulf of Tonkin in October 1966; 199

A-7As were delivered before production switched to the A-7B, which had an uprated engine. The USN took delivery of 198 examples. The next variant was the A-7D tactical fighter for the USAF, which went into action in Vietnam in October 1972; 459 were built. Also deployed to South-East Asia was the A-7E, a close support/interdiction variant developed for the US Navy. By the end of the conflict in Vietnam, A-7s had flown more than 100,000 combat missions. The aircraft was also used effectively during Operation Desert Storm in 1991. Corsair IIs were also operated by the Hellenic, Portuguese and Thai air forces.

Vought A-7E Corsair II

Type:	single-seat tactical fighter-bomber
Powerplant:	one 6464kg (14,255lb) thrust Allison TF41-1 (Rolls Royce Spey) turbofan
Performance:	speed 1123km/h (698mph); service ceiling 15,545m (51,000ft); range 1127km (700 miles)
Weights:	empty 8973kg (19,781lb); maximum take-off 19,050kg (42,000lb)
Dimensions:	wing span 11.8m (38ft 9in); length 14.06m (46ft 1.5in); height 4.9m (16ft 0.67in)
Armament:	one 20mm (0.79in) cannon; up to 6804kg (15,000lb) of munitions

The pilot of an A-7E lowers his arrester hook as he enters the pattern to land on the aircraft carrier USS *Ranger*.

An F-8 Crusader about to launch from the aircraft carrier USS *Constellation*.

The prototype XF8U-1 flew on 25 March 1955 and exceeded Mach One on its maiden flight, powered by a Pratt & Whitney J57 engine. The first production F8U-1 flew on 30 September 1955, and completed carrier trials in April 1956. The aircraft went into service as the F8U-1 in the following December. The F8U-1E (F-8B) version had a larger nose radome and limited all-weather capability. A reconnaissance version, the F8U-1P (RF-8A) was used for fast low-level reconnaissance over Vietnam. The F8U-2 (F-8C) was an improved version with a J57-P-16 turbojet, and flew in December 1967. It carried four Sidewinder AAMs as well as its cannon armament and had an improved fire control system. The F8U-2N (F-8D) Crusader, which first flew in February 1960, had an all-weather capability and an afterburning engine. The F-8H was a refurbished version. The last Crusader variant to carry the old US Service nomenclature was the F8U-2NE (F-8E), which was basically similar to the F-8D but with more advanced search and fire control radar equipment, the F-8J being an upgraded model. The F-8E(FN) was a version for the French Navy.

Vought F-8E Crusader

Type:	single-seat carrier-borne fighter
Powerplant:	one 8165kg (18,000lb) thrust Pratt & Whitney J57 P-20 turbojet
Performance:	maximum speed 1800km/h (1120mph) at 12,192m (40,000ft); service ceiling 17,983m (40,000ft); combat range 966km (600 miles)
Weights:	empty 9038kg (19,925lb); maximum take-off 15,422kg (34,000lb)
Dimensions:	wing span 10.72m (35ft 2in); length 16.61m (54ft 6in); height 4.80m (15ft 9in)
Armament:	four 20mm (0.79in) cannon; various combinations of rockets, bombs and ASMs

An F-8E (FN) Crusader of the French Navy, a split second from landing.

A search and rescue Whirlwind pictured in Snowdonia, Wales, in the 1970s.

In 1952–53 the Royal Navy took delivery of 25 Sikorsky S-55 helicopters, and some of these were assigned to the Navy's first anti-submarine helicopter squadron, No 706. Licence manufacture of the type was undertaken by Westland Aircraft, and initially two licence-built versions were produced, the HAR-1 for the Navy and the HAR-2 for the RAF; both saw service during the communist insurgency in Malaya. Production later standardized on the Whirlwind Series 3, fitted with a 783kW (1050hp) Bristol Siddeley Gnome shaft turbine engine. The Whirlwind Mk 9 Gnome conversion was used for training, rescue and general duties by the Royal Navy, while the HAR.Mk.10 was a new-build version for the RAF. The HAR.10, first delivered in 1961, saw operational service as a transport helicopter in Indonesia in the early 1960s, and in the Yemen before being withdrawn in 1967. The HAR.10 was also delivered to RAF Coastal Command in 1962, this version being armed with two air-to-surface missiles on each side of the fuselage. The Whirlwind HCC.Mk.12, two of which were built, was a special variant for the Queen's Flight.

Westland Whirlwind HCC.Mk.12

Type:	general-purpose helicopter
Powerplant:	one 783kW (1050hp) Bristol Siddeley Gnome H.1000 shaft turbine engine mounted horizontally in nose compartment
Performance:	maximum speed 170km/h (106mph); service ceiling 5060m (16,600ft); range 480km (300 miles)
Weights:	empty 2246kg (4952lb); maximum take-off 3629kg (8000lb)
Dimensions:	main rotor diameter 16.2m (53ft); length of fuselage 13.46m (44ft 2in); height to top of rotor hub 4.03m (13ft 2.5in)
Capacity:	10 troops or six stretchers

A Whirlwind's crew practise winching a survivor from the sea to safety.

Ilyushin Il-28 Beagle

The influx of German aeronautical engineers into the Soviet Union at the end of World War II enabled the Russians to develop their first generation of jet aircraft with extraordinary speed. One such aircraft was the Il-28.

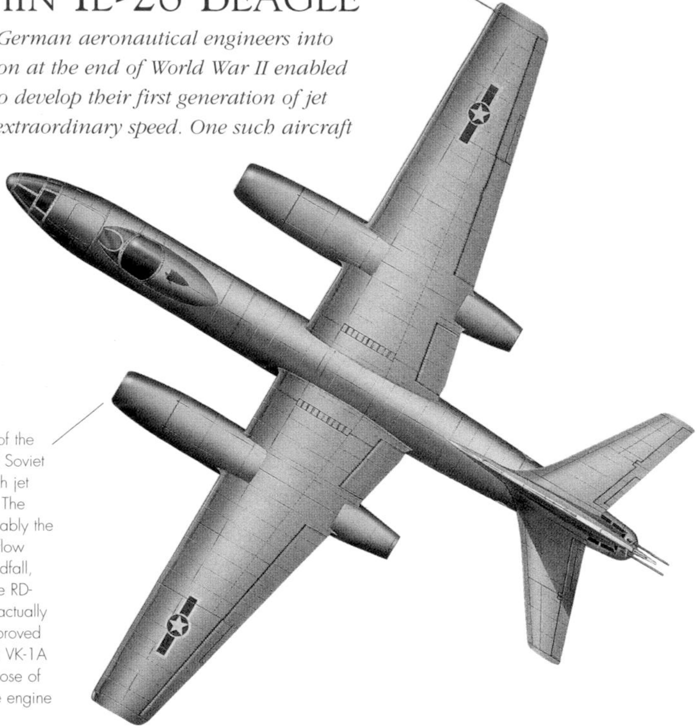

The Il-28 was one of the classic examples of Soviet exploitation of British jet engine technology. The Nene engine, probably the ultimate centrifugal-flow turbojet, was a windfall, being copied as the RD-45. The Il-28 was actually powered by an improved version, designated VK-1A (the initials being those of Vladimir Klimov, the engine manufacturer).

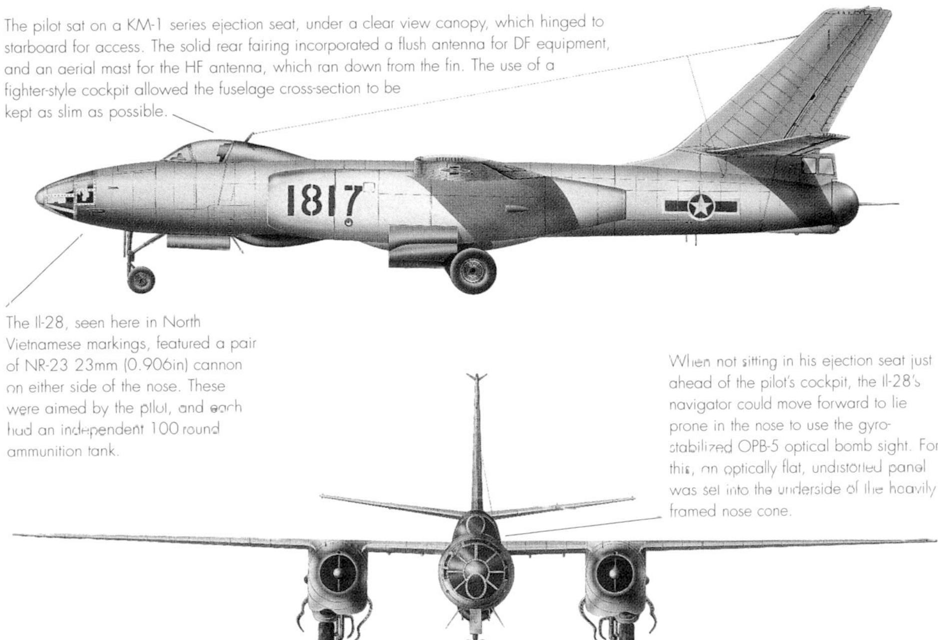

The pilot sat on a KM-1 series ejection seat, under a clear view canopy, which hinged to starboard for access. The solid rear fairing incorporated a flush antenna for DF equipment, and an aerial mast for the HF antenna, which ran down from the fin. The use of a fighter-style cockpit allowed the fuselage cross-section to be kept as slim as possible.

The Il-28, seen here in North Vietnamese markings, featured a pair of NR-23 23mm (0.906in) cannon on either side of the nose. These were aimed by the pilot, and each had an independent 100 round ammunition tank.

When not sitting in his ejection seat just ahead of the pilot's cockpit, the Il-28's navigator could move forward to lie prone in the nose to use the gyro-stabilized OPB-5 optical bomb sight. For this, an optically flat, undistorted panel was set into the underside of the heavily framed nose cone.

A Romanian Air Force MiG-21 streams its braking parachute on landing.

The initial production versions (MiG-21A and -B) were built only in limited numbers, being short-range day fighters with a comparatively light armament of two 30mm (1.19in) NR-30 cannon. But the next variant, the MiG-21F, carried two K-13 Atoll infra red homing AAMs and had an uprated Tumansky R-11 turbojet as well as improved avionics. The MiG-21F was the first major production version; it entered service in 1960 and was progressively modified and updated over the years that followed. In the early 1970s the MiG-21 was redesigned, re-emerging as the MiG-21B multi-role air superiority fighter and ground-attack version. This was followed by the MiG-21M and -N, with updated systems for air combat and ground attack. In its several versions the MiG-21 became the most widely used jet fighter in the world, being licence-built in India, Czechoslovakia and China, and equipping some 25 Soviet-aligned air forces. In Vietnam, the MiG-21 was the Americans' deadliest opponent. The MiG-21 received the NATO reporting name 'Fishbed'; a two-seat version, the MiG-21U, was called Mongol.

Mikoyan-Gurevich MiG-21M

Type:	single-seat multi-role combat aircraft
Powerplant:	one 7507kg (16,553lb) thrust Tumanskii R-25 turbojet
Performance:	maximum speed 2229km/h (1385mph) at 11,000m (36,090ft); service ceiling 17,500m (57,400ft); range 1160km (721 miles)
Weights:	empty 5200kg (11,466lb); maximum take-off 10,400kg (22,932lb)
Dimensions:	wing span 7.15m (23ft 5.5in); length 15.76m (51ft 8.5in); height 4.10m (13ft 5.5in)
Armament:	one 23mm (0.906in) twin-barrel cannon; four underwing pylons for 1500kg (3307lb) of munitions

In Romanian Air Force service the MiG-21 became known as the Lancer.

USSR/RUSSIA

MIKOYAN-GUREVICH MIG-29M

The appearance in the early 1980s of the MiG-29, with its superb agility and its apparent ability to perform combat manoeuvres that could not be matched by any aircraft in the West, came as an unpleasant surprise to NATO.

The MiG-29M has an increased-area horizontal tailplane, giving greater control authority in pitch (when both tailplanes are used symmetrically) and in roll (when used differentially). An inboard dogtooth discontinuity generates an airflow vortex, which keeps flow attached at high deflection angles.

Forty per cent of the MiG-29's lift is provided by its lift-generating centre fuselage and the aircraft is able to achieve angles of attack at least 70 per cent higher than earlier fighters.

Whereas the basic MiG-29 had a dedicated air-to-air radar in the shape of its N-019 (RLPK-29) 'Slot Black', the MiG-29M has a more versatile, modern multi-mode radar with multiple air-to-air and air-to-ground modes. The latter include terrain following and avoidance, real-beam or synthetic aperture mapping, target designation for air-to-surface missiles, and a range of navigation options.

A wide variety of ordnance has been displayed on the MiG-29M. This example is carrying Kh-31 defence suppression missiles on the inboard pylons and R-73 (AA-11 Archer) and R-77 (AA-12 Adder) AAMs inboard.

The MiG-29 Fulcrum was designed in response to the F-15 and its naval counterpart, the Grumman F-14 Tomcat. MiG-29 design emphasis from the start was on very high manoeuvrability and the ability to destroy targets at distances of between 200m (660ft) and 60km (32nm). The aircraft has an RP-29 pulse-Doppler

The MiG-29's incredible degree of manoeuvrability surprised the West.

radar capable of detecting targets at around 100km (62 miles) against a background of ground clutter. Fire control and mission computers link the radar with a laser rangefinder and infra red search/track sensor, in conjunction with a helmet-mounted target designator. The radar can track ten targets simultaneously, and the system allows the MiG-29 to approach and engage targets without emitting detectable radar or radio signals. The MiG-29K is a navalized version, the MiG-29M is a variant with advanced fly-by-wire systems, and the MiG-29UB is a two-seat operational trainer. The MiG-29 was allocated the NATO reporting name Fulcrum after it became operational in 1985.

Mikoyan-Gurevich MiG-29M

Type:	single-seat air superiority fighter
Powerplant:	two 9409kg (20,747lb) thrust Sarkisov RD-33K turbofans
Performance:	Maximum speed 2300km/h (1430mph) at 11,000m (36,090ft); service ceiling 17,000m (55,774ft); range 1500km (932 miles)
Weights:	empty 10,900kg (24,035lb); maximum take-off 18,500kg (40,785lb)
Dimensions:	wing span 11.36m (37ft 3.67in); length 17.32m (56ft 10in), height 7.78m (25ft 6.67in)
Armament:	one 30mm (1.19in) cannon; eight external hardpoints for up to 4500kg (9921lb) of munitions

The MiG-29's main engine intakes could be closed for ground manoeuvring.

USSR/RUSSIA

First flown on 16 September 1975, the MiG-31 (known by the NATO reporting name Foxhound) entered production in 1975 and became operational in 1982, replacing MiG-23s and Su-15s. The aircraft is a two-seat, all-weather, all-altitude interceptor designed to be guided automatically to its targets and to engage

This MiG-31 displays a formidable array of air-to-air weaponry.

them under ground control. In a typical mission profile, an interception would be made by a flight of four aircraft, the leader being linked to the AK-RLDN ground radar guidance network and the other three linked to the leader by APD-518 digital datalink. This arrangement permits a line abreast radar sweep covering a zone some 900km (485nm) wide. One variant of the MiG-31, the MiG-31D, is a dedicated anti-satellite aircraft. The MiG-31M was an upgraded variant, development starting in 1984. Modifications included improved engines with modified nozzles; a one-piece rounded windscreen with small side windows installed in the rear cockpit; a wider and deeper dorsal spine containing additional fuel; more rounded wingtips, with flush dielectric areas at front and rear; taller fins with larger, curved root extensions; and a completely updated electronics suite.

Mikoyan-Gurevich MiG-31M

Type:	two-seat long-range interceptor
Powerplant:	two 15,500kg (34,178lb) thrust Soloviev D-30F6 turbofans
Performance:	maximum speed 3000km/h (1865mph) at 17,500m (57,400ft); service ceiling 20,600m (67,600ft); combat radius 1400km (870 miles) with weapons load
Weights:	empty 21,825kg (48,115lb); maximum take-off 46,200kg (101,850lb)
Dimensions:	wing span 13.46m (44ft 2in); length 22.68m (74ft 5.25in); height 6.15m (20ft 2.25in)
Armament:	up to 10 AAMs of various types

The Foxhound was developed to intercept air-launched cruise missiles.

Mil Mi-24

Code-named 'Hind' by NATO, the Mil Mi-24 is one of the world's most potent attack helicopters, and saw extensive service in Russia's fruitless war in Afghanistan.

The Hind-E is armed with a four-barrelled 12.7mm (0.50in) machine gun in a chin turret, carrying 1470 rounds of ammunition. Also carried are four AT-6 Spiral anti-armour missile launch tubes on pairs on the endplate pylons, with gun pods on the inboard underwing pylons. These gun pods each contain a GSh-23L 23mm (0.906in) cannon.

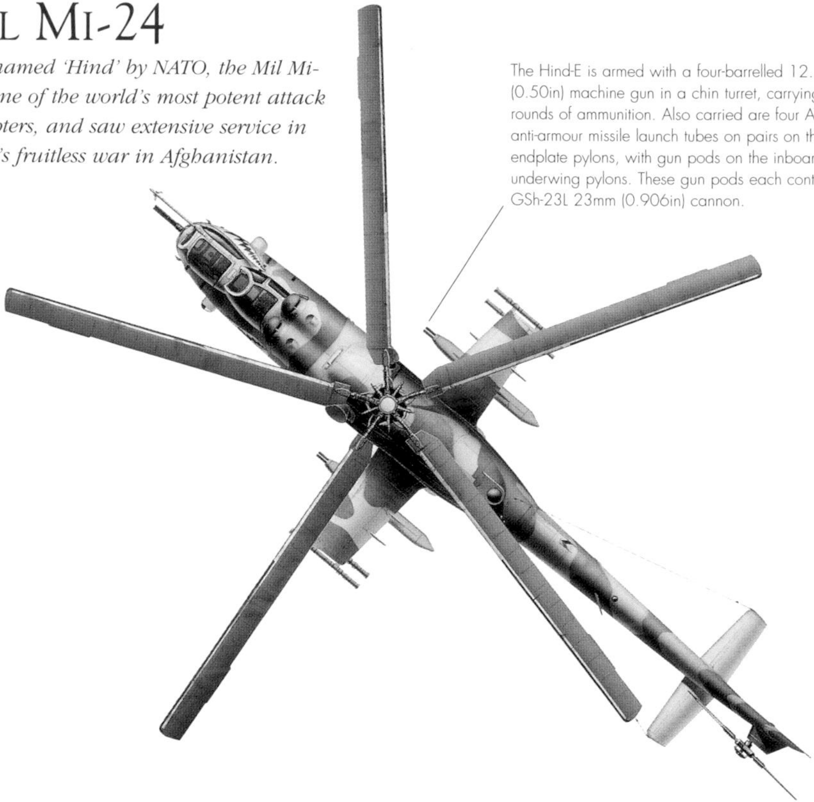

The standard under-nose electro-optical package is carried to starboard with a new fixed Shturm V guidance antenna in a fixed fairing with hemispherical radome to port.

This aircraft is painted in standard Soviet ground forces aviation camouflage, with serial numbers applied in small white characters to the tailboom, and with the national marking on the rear fuselage sides.

Seen here is a shark-mouthed Mi-24V Hind-E of the Polish 56th Assault Helicopter Regiment, Inowroclaw. In Polish service the helicopter is known as the Mi-24W. Poland received 16 Mi-24Ws, and the one aircraft that was lost in service was replaced.

The Mi-24 was a development of the earlier Mi-8. It is a close counterpart to the American AH-64 Apache, but unlike western assault helicopters it is capable of transporting up to eight troops. The Mi-24 features a five-blade main rotor mounted on the fuselage midsection; mounted directly below it are stubby wings

The Mi-24 is one of the world's most potent attack helicopters.

that carry the helicopter's main armament. The original Hind-A's fuselage consisted of a large, oval-shaped body with a glazed cockpit; this was modified in the later Hind-D to incorporate tandem bubble canopies and a chin-mounted gun turret. The swept-back tapered tail fin carries a three-blade rotor, which on some models is mounted on the starboard side. Each of the stub wings has three weapons hardpoints. These wings provide up to 28% of the helicopter's lift in forward flight. In a steep banking turn at slower airspeeds, the loss of lift on the lower wing can result in excessive roll, which is countered by increasing airspeed. Because of this and other factors, not least its size and weight, the Mi-24 is not especially manoeuvrable. Including the CIS, the Mi-24 is used by at least 34 countries.

Mil Mi-24E 'Hind E'

Type:	assault and transport helicopter
Powerplant:	two 2200 Isotov TV-3-117V turboshaft engines
Performance:	maximum speed 335km/h (208mph); service ceiling 4500m (14,763ft); range 450km (279 miles)
Weights:	empty 8500kg (18,742lb); maximum take-off 11,500kg (25,358lb)
Dimensions:	main rotor diameter 17.3m (56ft 9in); fuselage length 17.5m (57ft 5in); height 6.5m (21ft 4in)
Armament:	one four-barrelled 12.7mm (0.50in) machine gun; two GSh-23L 23mm (0.906in) cannon pods and four AT-6 Spiral anti-tank missile launch tubes

A photo showing the Hind's stub wings, with four anti-armour rocket pods.

A two-seat version of the Flanker, the Su-27 UB, at the Farnborough Air Show.

Like the F-15, the Sukhoi Su-27 is a dual-role aircraft. In addition to its primary air superiority task it was designed to escort Su-24 Fencer strike aircraft on deep penetration missions. The first prototype, designated T10-1, flew on 20 May 1977. The T10-1 did not meet requirements and had numerous problems; the second prototype, the T10-2, crashed and killed its pilot. In 1981 a new prototype appeared, after much redesign - the T10S. It was this aircraft that evolved into the Su-27. Full-scale production of the Su-27P Flanker-B air defence fighter began in 1980, but the aircraft did not become fully operational until 1984. Like its contemporary, the MiG-29 Fulcrum, the Su-27 combines a wing swept at 40 degrees with highly swept wing root extensions, underslung engines with wedge intakes, and twin fins. The combination of modest wing sweep with highly swept root extensions, is designed to enhance manoeuvrability and generate lift, making it possible to achieve quite extraordinary angles of attack. The Su-27UB Flanker-C is a two-seat training version. The Sukhoi Su-35, derived from the Flanker-B, is a second-generation version with improved agility and enhanced operational capability.

Sukhoi Su-27 Flanker-B

Type: single-seat air superiority fighter
Powerplant: two 12,500kg (27,562lb) thrust Lyulka AL-31F turbofans
Performance: maximum speed 2500km/h (1552mph) at altitude; service ceiling 18,000m (59,055ft); range 4000km (2485 miles)
Weights: empty 20,748kg (45,741lb); maximum take-off 30,000kg (66,138lb)
Dimensions: wing span 14.70m (48ft 2.67in); length 21.94m (71ft 11.5in); height 6.36m (20ft 10.25in)
Armament: one 30mm (1.19in) cannon; ten external hardpoints for various AAMs

The Su-27 Flanker proved more than a match for its western contemporaries.

A Tupolev Tu-22 Blinder pictured in a somewhat derelict condition.

The Tupolev Tu-22 Blinder, designed as a supersonic successor to the Badger, was first seen publicly at the Tushino air display in 1961. Those Tu-22s were pre-series trials aircraft, and first deliveries of the type to the Soviet Strategic Air Force were not made until the following year. The first operational version, code-named Blinder-A, was produced in limited numbers only, because its range of about 3100km (1926 miles) fell short of strategic requirements. The second variant, the Tu-22K Blinder-B, was equipped with a flight refuelling probe; 12 aircraft were supplied to Iraq and 24 to Libya. One of the Iraqi aircraft was shot down during an attack on the Iranian capital, Tehran, in 1981; others were used to attack Kurdish villages accused of harbouring insurgents hostile to the regime of Saddam Hussein. The Libyan aircraft made several attacks on Tanzania in support of Ugandan forces, and in 1986 a single aircraft bombed N'Djamena airport in Chad in retaliation for a French raid on Ouadi Doum. The Tu-22R Blinder-C was a dedicated maritime reconnaissance variant, about 60 of which were built, and the Tu-22P Blinder-E was an ECM aircraft.

Tu-22P Blinder E

Type:	electronic warfare support aircraft with three or four crew
Powerplant:	two 16,000kg (35,280lb) thrust Koliesov VD-7M turbojets
Performance:	maximum speed 1487km/h (924mph) at 6000m (19,685ft); service ceiling 18,300m (60,040ft); range 3100km (1926 miles)
Weights:	empty 40,000kg (88,200lb); maximum take-off 84,000kg (185,200lb)
Dimensions:	wing span 23.75m (77ft 11in); length 40.53m (132ft 11.67in); height 10.67m (35ft)
Armament:	one 23mm (0.906in) cannon.

A Tu-22 leads a formation of MiG-21s in a flypast to mark the 50th anniversary of the October Revolution, July 1967.

Tupolev Tu-22M Backfire

For many years, western intelligence experts tried to establish the true role of the Tu-22M Backfire bomber. It was a long time before they realized it presented the biggest threat ever to the convoy routes between the United States and Europe.

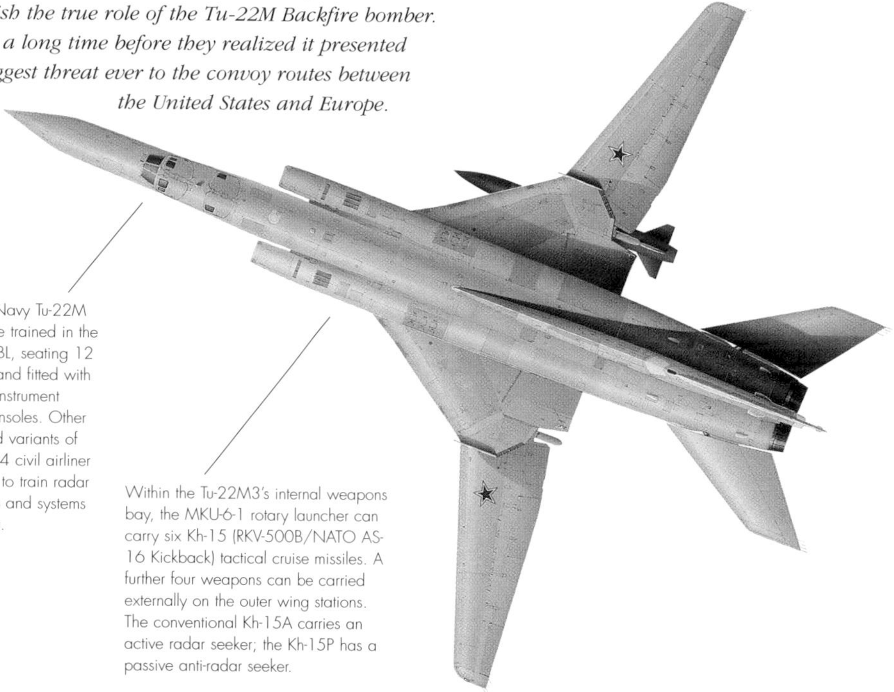

Russian Navy Tu-22M crews are trained in the Tu-134UBL, seating 12 trainees and fitted with Tu-22M instrument panel consoles. Other converted variants of the Tu-134 civil airliner are used to train radar operators and systems operators.

Within the Tu-22M3's internal weapons bay, the MKU-6-1 rotary launcher can carry six Kh-15 (RKV-500B/NATO AS-16 Kickback) tactical cruise missiles. A further four weapons can be carried externally on the outer wing stations. The conventional Kh-15A carries an active radar seeker; the Kh-15P has a passive anti-radar seeker.

This Tu-22M3 is carrying a Kh-22 (NATO Kitchen) anti-shipping missile. Following a Mach 2.5 steep terminal phase dive, a single Kh-22 can tear a $20m^2$ (215 sq ft) hole in the side of a ship before burning its way 12m (39ft) into the vessel, ensuring the destruction of the internal bulkheads. The standard Kh-22 carries a 1000kg (2205lb) high explosive warhead. Kh-22P/N variants carry a 3.5kT nuclear warhead and have a range of 550km (340 miles) when launched at high altitude.

The Tu-22M3's defensive armament is provided by a single twin-barrelled GSh-23 cannon in the tail barbette. Ammunition supply is 1200 rounds of PIKS infra red decoy and PRLS chaff. The gun is aimed using the PRS-4 Krypton or supplementary TP-1 TV sight.

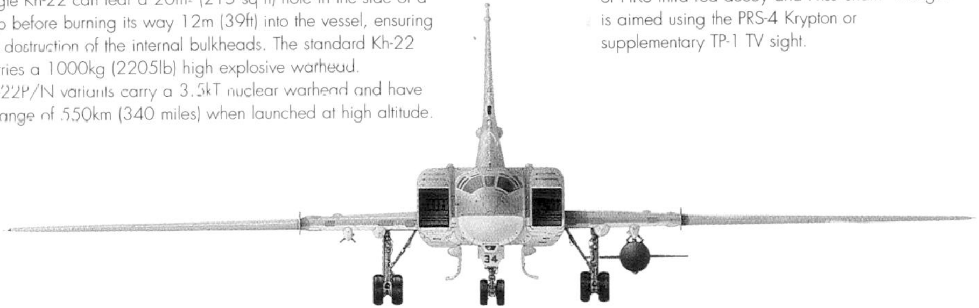

TUPOLEV TU-160 BLACKJACK

The concept of the supersonic bomber dates back to the 1950s, but it was not until the 1980s that it became truly viable, first with America's Rockwell B-1 and then with Russia's Tu-160, code-named Blackjack by NATO.

Most of the aircraft's fuel is housed in the large wing centre-section, and is sufficient to provide a range of about 14,000km (8694 miles). Mission endurance is further extended by in-flight refuelling, a probe for which is located in the nose ahead of the cockpit. This is retractable, covered by long double doors when not in use.

Wearing a white paint scheme, presumably as protection against nuclear flash (like Britain's V-bomber force of the early 1960s), this Tu-160 was part of the 184th Heavy Bomber Regiment, based at Priluki in the Ukraine.

The Tu-160 is flown by a crew of four, comprising two pilots seated side-by-side, and two navigators behind. One of the latter is known as the 'navigator-operator' and is responsible for aiming the weapons, while the other navigator is responsible for en-route navigation. All crew members sit on K-36 upward firing ejection seats.

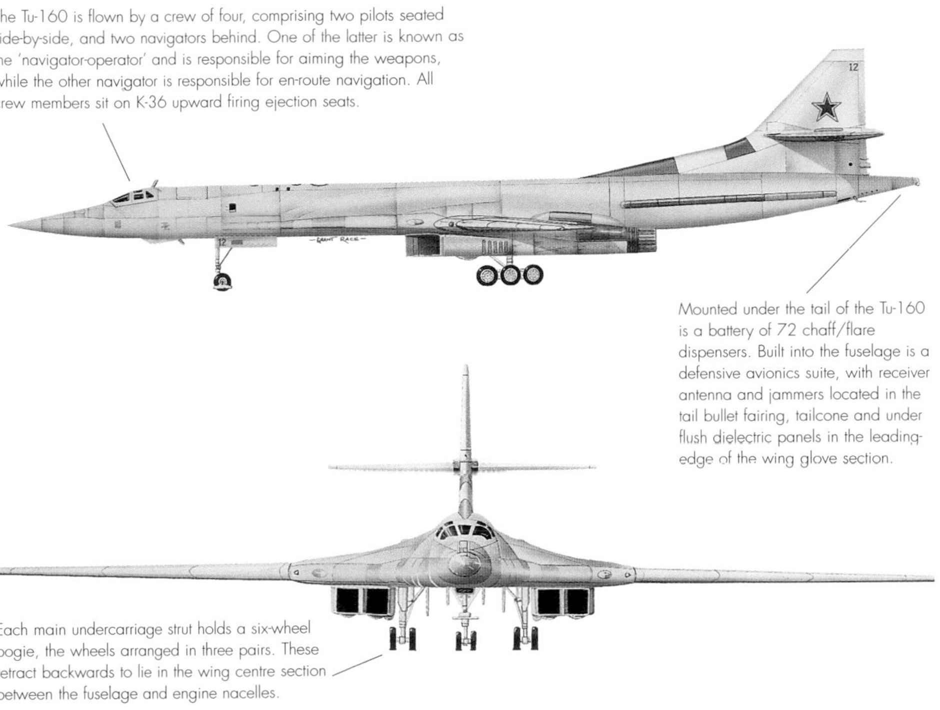

Mounted under the tail of the Tu-160 is a battery of 72 chaff/flare dispensers. Built into the fuselage is a defensive avionics suite, with receiver antenna and jammers located in the tail bullet fairing, tailcone and under flush dielectric panels in the leading-edge of the wing glove section.

Each main undercarriage strut holds a six-wheel bogie, the wheels arranged in three pairs. These retract backwards to lie in the wing centre section between the fuselage and engine nacelles.

Ukraine's Tu-160s have rarely flown since the break-up of the Soviet Union.

The Tu-160 emerged from a multi-mission bomber competition in which the competitors included a Tupolev proposal (using elements from the Tu-144 supersonic airliner), a Sukhoi design based on the T-4 aircraft, and the Myasishchev M-18. The last design was considered to be the most promising, and the development project was handed over to the Tupolev Design Bureau, as the Tupolev organization was thought to be the best equipped to handle this complex project. The Tu-160, as the design was redesignated, first flew on 19 December 1981, but one of the two prototypes was lost in an accident. Comparable to but much larger than the Rockwell B-1B, the TU-160 entered production in 1984 and the first operational aircraft were deployed in May 1987. Thirty-six were operational in 1989 (out of a planned total of 100) with the Soviet Air Force, divided between the 184th Air Regiment in the Ukraine and the 121st Air Regiment at Engels Air Base. The Ukraine-based aircraft were eventually returned to Russia, along with 600 air-launched missiles, as part of a deal that involved paying off a commercial debt.

Tupolev Tu-160 Blackjack-A

Type:	strategic bomber with four crew
Powerplant:	four 25,000kg (55,125lb) thrust Kuznetsov NK-321 turbofans
Performance:	maximum speed 2000km/h (1243mph) at 11,000m (36,089ft); service ceiling 18,300m (60,040ft); range 14,000km (8694 miles)
Weights:	110,000kg (242,550lb); maximum take-off 275,000kg (606,261lb)
Dimensions:	wing span 55.70m (182ft 9in) spread; 35.60m (116ft 9in) swept; length 54.10m (177ft 6in), height 13.10m (43ft)
Armament:	up to 16,500kg (36,383lb) of munitions

Only a small number of 'Blackjacks' remain in service, due to the huge cost.

INDEX

Note: page numbers in *italics* refer to illustrations. Page references in **bold** type indicate major references